To Anthea
Words can

The Depth of Love

How deeply you are

appreciated ?

Much love,

Axxx

p.ii

<u>Books by GR</u>

3 bks + Runt

SIL – Book 1
DOL – Book 2
Opening The Heart – Bk 3

The Depth of Love

spiritual transitions

Gretchen Korzaan

SALT RIVER

TUPPANY BOOKS
is an imprint of Salt River Publishing
Phoenix, Arizona
www.SaltRiverPublishing.com

FIRST EDITION 2020
20   5 4 3 2 1   I
ISBN 978-1-946051-20-2

Publisher discount at
SaltRiverPublishing.com

Contents

The cracked pot

Intuitive and talented artist Cynthia Spring has captured the essence of *The Depth of Love* in her wonderful cover.

The cracked pot symbolizes new beginnings – those transitions that leave rational and logical thought behind and allow us to bravely step out, forging new pathways of thinking and actions that will lead us towards the Light – that Lotus within – the ocean of the Lord's love.

The cracked pot also still functions, watering the surrounding flowers and protecting the core of our being. It is almost like the chrysalis that protects the caterpillar as it transforms into a butterfly.

Changes are happening deep inside our being, and at every step we are being cared for and surrounded by the Lord's love.

Enjoy the journey, dear friends, for the mystics tell us that His love will transform the soul and make it whole.

Transitions

I chose the title for this book, *The Depth of Love*, for many reasons. The saints and mystics tell us love is the anchor, the mainstay of our lives. They say when the heart is filled with love all things become possible – we will find solutions to even the most difficult situations we may face, and those solutions will give us the strength and courage to continue to seek and explore.

The mystics tells us that the nature of God is love, that he is an ocean of love. How do we find this love? As seekers after the truth, we need to dive in and explore the depth of love from every angle, so we can understand and grasp what the saints and mystics have come to share with us – that our true identity is the soul, and this world is not our true home. Maharaj Charan Singh states:

It is the Lord who, in his benevolence, has given us this rare chance, and it is for us to take full advantage of it. We must continue to search for our true home as long as we live.[*]

---

*For sources of all quotes, see Notes section.

3

The subtitle, *Spiritual Transitions*, felt appropriate because change is the one constant in our lives. We may feel a myriad of things when transitions affect our lives. There may be anxiety or fear of the unknown, a feeling of release, perhaps a weight lifted, or questions about how our life will be affected – will we have the courage to face the future?

It may help us to realize that transitions build the base for spiritual growth. Without change, the mystics say we cannot grow to become one with the Lord. We are on a journey to God, my friends. Hafiz puts it this way when he encourages us:

Like a great film or play everyone should see –
BEHOLD THYSELF.
Hints of your beauty the mountains have.
The enchanting complexities of the coral reefs
Are pale to a golden candle in our heart.
What moves in any ocean moves through us.
A thousand kinds of music play every hour
That you orchestrate.
Let the next ticket you buy help seat you in
Front of ... your soul.

The essence

Remember when you were little and looked at the stars or the moon and your eyes lit up in wonder? As we grew older, we still enjoyed, but started questioning where the planets, stars, sun and moon came from and what they were made of. We gathered information to help us understand their origin.

Now, as seekers after truth, the desire to know God personally has awakened that yearning to understand the essence of our soul. And the questions come again – why are we here, who are we, is there life after death, what is our true purpose, and so on.

The saints and mystics come to help us find answers to our questions and show us the way to realize the soul's birthright, its divine nature.

The purpose of this little book is to encourage us to dive into love from the mystics' point of view. There are stories, quotes, and poems from mystics, teachers and saints from all ages, all cultures and many different religions, both past and present, that show us that God's truth is for everyone seeking to unwrap the mysteries that veil the soul. These spiritual teachers come to guide us in our search for God-realization.

Enjoy the journey, my friends!

1

Awakening

Have you ever woken up mystified, feeling that something was different – something that you couldn't define or understand? This profound sense of some intrinsic, deep and vital change seemed to surround you completely and you felt compelled to explore why this was happening. Nothing seemed to have shifted in your outer life, so perhaps you felt it was an inner revelation.

How can we understand what was going on? Opening a page of the inner book of life we turn to what the mystics and saints teach.

The saints and mystics come to explain to all of us that life is much more than what we see, hear, smell, touch, taste and feel. They encourage us to awaken our inner vision to explore what lies within. They say that to gain the essence of spirituality we have to go beyond the intellect.

This body is transient and subject to decay, wading through the shifting sands of time and space and having a limited span of existence. The saints come to help us realize that this human body is simply a covering for the soul, which is eternal and deathless. They tell us our sole purpose is to realize that we are souls waking up.

Hafiz tells us:

What is this precious love and laughter
Budding in our hearts?
It is the glorious sound
Of a soul waking up!

This great Sufi poet and mystic encourages us to celebrate even the most ordinary experiences of life as precious divine gifts. He invites us to 'awake awhile' and listen to the delightful music of God's laughter.

Let us explore the act of awakening. What does it mean to the soul, and how does it take place?

In *Spiritual Link* magazine, there is a quote from a contemporary mystic:

Our spiritual development is not a race, it is a gentle unfolding of infinite beauty.

The saints and mystics tell us the soul is an amazing, infinite particle of the divine essence of God. Each day, each breath can shape us and redefine our inner terrain. The saints share that understanding simply grows and grows as the spirit awakens to the richness and wealth of its spiritual heritage. This treasure is there now, in us, for us.

The mystics tell us not to be in a hurry, but to explore, journey, and experience the depth of this spiritual love in each moment. It does not happen instantly. The saints say it takes time for most of us, as the rust of eons of living must be removed to realize God at the highest level.

Hafiz shares with us so beautifully:

I would like to remove some rocks from your field
so that you can plant more wheat.
And those hills I see that are part of you,
I have some trees in mind for them
And flowering grasses,
So that you won't erode when the elements pour.
Are we not lovers?
Cannot I speak to you like this?
Do I need to ask your permission

To hitch up my ox and sing to him
As I improve your vast terrain?
The title to your heart came to my office.
In looking at it a great interest in your soul developed.
The care of your soul became mine.
So I would like to remove some stones
from your meadows,
Then an orchard you could grow,
And the world, and the world then
Will come to taste your riches.

Patience is one of the tag words that become part of our day-to-day vocabulary of living. This gentle unfolding of infinite beauty takes time and effort on our part. We are so used to quick results that we often fail to see what is right inside of us – we are in too great a hurry to be open and receptive to the changes that help us to see. The mystics continually tell us to expand our horizons, to spread beyond this outer world into the inner – to open to the true reality and awaken to the richness that is soul!

Baba Jaimal Singh says:

The reality of life is the soul, my son....The stream
of divine knowledge is flowing, so the current of
mercy is about to come, and is already coming.

What does the reality of life mean? Why are we here and what is our true purpose?

The mystics and saints explain to us that we are spiritual beings, our true essence being the soul. They tell us this life is transitory and impermanent. They try to guide us, to help us understand the immeasurable gift of this human body and what it can mean to the soul if we open ourselves to the possibilities.

It requires commitment and action on our part – to study, to seek, to grasp this concept that we are spiritual beings who have been given the chance to realize our true nature now, not sometime in the future or after death.

This letter from one brother to another, shares deep feelings about his life's journey:

For the past twenty years I have been preparing... I know my solitude and seclusion has caused concern. Please forgive me and find peace in the knowledge that these have been my most focused and devotional years. I feel honoured, humbled and blessed by God's grace to have been given the great blessing of finding a teacher who inspired and taught me to love the one true God.

We humans have the rare privilege and opportunity to find God within our body, which is truly the temple of the Lord and the top of creation. He is 'nearer than the royal vein', just as we are told, yet unfortunately most are looking elsewhere.

Through his Word, Holy Spirit, Shabd, Hukam, Kalma or Name (all attributive words for the Lord), he is the essence of the entire creation – yet timeless, immortal and detached he remains.

Seek and you will find his door. Knock and it will be opened for you.

The seeking and knocking are what makes us human. God has placed the path to him within our body. The path takes a lifetime of patient sincere knocking, with our ego and hearts in our hands as an offering. These we have to surrender.

May his patience, his compassion, his grace, his love and his wisdom fill your hearts always.

This human birth is invaluable, the mystics teach; each moment more precious than all of the wealth in the world, for it offers us the opportunity to meet the Lord.

Step-by-step, if we follow the instructions the saints and mystics share, we can realize God now, before death, while in this human body. Practice, patience and perseverance, the mystics tell us, will show the way to this inner realization.

Only human beings have the sense of discrimination, or what the saints call vivek. We can differentiate right from wrong and make choices accordingly. The choices we make can take us closer to the Lord or immerse us more deeply in the world and its illusions.

The mystics tell us that this is the time to meet the Lord, and they caution us to use our time wisely when they say it is a rare and valuable opportunity. Kabir says:

> *Rare is the human birth, it occurs not again and again,*
> *Like the ripe fruit, which falls from the tree*
> *And can never rejoin with the branch.*

We are on a journey to God, my friends, and we don't want to let this life slip through our fingers. We seek to grasp the essence and become that which we are seeking. As Maharaj Sawan Singh tells us:

My home is within you and I am also within you. The outward homes are of clay and are perishable. The real permanent home is within. I wish you could come up and see me there.

2

Destiny

The mystics tell us that this world is a place of action and reaction, of karmic destiny – you reap what you have sown through your past choices. What actions we take now in this human form can turn us in the right direction. The light of God's word shines behind the eyes of every living being, so now is the time for the soul to become aware, conscious of its divine heritage.

The dictionary defines awareness as the state of being conscious of something. More specifically, it is the ability to directly know and perceive, to feel.

Why are we here? To gain the ability to seek and find the truth that lies within. The mystics tell us that our life revolves around love – a divine spiritual love that cannot be described in words. Through their teachings and encouragement, they help us understand love, absorb love, and merge into love.

In the *Book of Mirdad* the entire focus of why we are here as human beings is expressed simply and beautifully:

You love that you may learn to live;
You live so that you may learn to Love.
No other lesson is required of man.
And what is it to love but for the lover
To absorb forever the Beloved
So that the twain be one?

The mystics come to help us tap into that spiritual love. They are teachers, friends and poets who share their vast wealth of personal experience with us and encourage us with each step. What they wish for us is to enter the depth of love – the unlimited wealth the mystics tell us is our birthright.

Dnyaneshwar gives us an idea of what a mystic is:

Mystics –
gardens of wish-fulfilling trees,
villages of dazzling, wish-granting jewels
whose words are a living ocean of nectar –
spotless moons and heatless suns

are these virtuous ones, our true family:
May they be loved by all through all time.

The mystics and saints come to open our hearts
and help us see and experience the reality that
is soul. Mirdad tells us:

Set no limits to yourselves. Spread out until
there are no regions where you are not.
Spread out until the whole world be wherever
you may chance to be. Spread out till you
meet God where'er you meet yourselves.
Spread out! Spread out!

Accepting and appreciating who and what you are
regardless of what anyone else may think helps
us to be open to the possibilities.

A personal note I'd like to share: One day, after
having to unexpectedly leave a way of life and
make a major move, I was feeling really blue
and disheartened. I felt stomped on and unsure
of myself. As a single parent it was staggering to
think of what life might bring and whether I would
be capable of dealing with all of the uncertainty.

Then, as I rounded the corner of a building, I saw
a climbing rosebush. I stopped for a moment to
breathe in the fragrance and appreciate its simple

beauty, and had a pivotal moment – a moment that changed my life. I realized that it didn't matter what anyone else thought or did, or even what happened in the future: God loved me and He would see me through.

I can't tell you how many times I have thought of that moment and it has helped me through many difficult times.

Remember that beautiful song by Donovan – "The Little Church:"

If you want your dream to be, take your time, go slowly.

Do few things but do them well, heartfelt work grows purely.

If you want to live life free, take your time,

go slowly...

Day by day, stone by stone, build your secret slowly.

Day by day, you'll grow too, you'll know heaven's glory.

We are all so blessed to have this opportunity in a human form. Every breath becomes precious as we grow to understand that we are a drop in the vast ocean of His love.

The mystics unveil to us the ways we can participate and experience this love in action in our daily lives. Hafiz describes it beautifully in "The Great Work:"

Love is the great work though every heart is an apprentice that slaves beneath the city of Light (our worldly destiny). This wondrous trade, this magnificent throne your soul is destined for – you should not have to think much about it. Is it not clear an apprentice needs a teacher who himself has charmed the universe to reveal its wonders inside his cup? Happiness is the great work, though every heart must first become a student to see who really knows about Love.

The saints say that to become masters of spirituality, we must first become students – open the doors of our heart and experiment, practice and question until we start to understand what divine love is.

A question was asked of Maharaj Charan Singh:

Q. I have read in books that love may be generated to any degree, but it doesn't tell one just how to do that... How can we generate that love?

A. You can be receptive to the Lord's grace. When it is raining, if you keep the cup right-side up, it will collect water. So you can be receptive to his grace. The Lord has given us this environment, this facility, this company in which we can strengthen each other's love and be helpful to each other. These are all a means for generating love, so we can be receptive to all these things.

But still, everything is in the hands of the Lord. He creates his own love in us. We then feel that we love him or that we are separated from him and we want to become one with him. He's the one who is pulling us from within. That is entirely in his hands. Unless he gives us the means, we can never generate that love ourselves.

Meditation generates love. Meditation creates that pang in you, that desire in you to become one with the Father. Meditation makes you realize that life is worthless without Him... When God wants you to love him, he will give you that love; but it comes by meditation, as instructed by the living master.

However we choose to turn to God, whether through prayer, meditation remembrance or simply speaking quietly to him, love will be generated.

The mystics tell us that we need a teacher, someone who has travelled the inner path and can guide us through the intricate twists and turns of destiny.

Whoever our teacher is, whether they are a priest, guru, dervish, well-wisher or friend, it is helpful to develop a relationship of trust with them. They will help us learn about our spiritual goal.

The mystics tell us we need to focus on the inner reality, rather than this outward shadow-show called life. The saints teach that those who allow themselves to dare to turn to love will be infinitely rewarded.

3

The worth of a soul

All saints and mystics tell us how precious we are to the Lord who resides within each soul. Rumi puts it this way:

You are more precious than heaven and earth. Why sell yourself at little price, being so precious in God's eyes?

The mystics say they are here to provide us with the opportunity to grow inwardly and will continuously shower grace upon each of our moments if we strive to understand.

They tell us the Lord's love will infuse us with the desire to learn the true purpose of this human birth. The saints and mystics tell us the main reason that they come into this creation is to teach us to learn how to love and be responsive to our true identity – that of soul.

Mirdad tells us specifically:

*Man is a God in swaddling bands. Time is a
swaddling band. Space is a swaddling band.
Flesh is a swaddling band, and likewise
all the senses and the things perceivable
therewith. The Mother (the teacher, the
mystic) knows too well that the swaddling
bands are not the babe. The babe, however,
knows it not. Man is too conscious yet of his
swaddles, which change from day to day and
from age to age. Hence is his consciousness
ever in flux; and hence his word which is
his consciousness expressed is never clear
and definite of meaning; and hence his
understanding is in fog; and hence is his life
out of balance. It is confusion...This is man's
destiny – to fight (through meditation, prayer,
remembrance) and in the end to wake (to
God-realization).*

We have our work cut out for us. We cannot simply
find the teachings we need in books or discourses;
we must imbibe these teachings in our hearts and
then act with honest intention. If each of our days
holds a sincere effort to expand the truth within
and awaken to the spiritual possibilities, there
are treasures waiting to be discovered!

The mystics tell us the Word, Audible Life Stream,
Sound Current, Shabd and Nam (Name) are part

of our very being – we just need to seek them out
to awaken to soul consciousness.

We have to ask ourselves, what is real in life. There
is no dearth of knowledge, but true understanding,
the saints tell us, comes when you know – when we
personally experience reality within. Rumi says:

> *O lovers, where are you going? Who are you*
> *looking for? Your Beloved is right here.... He*
> *lives in your own neighborhood. His face is*
> *veiled.... He hides behind scenes calling for*
> *you while you search and lose yourself in*
> *the wilderness and desert. Cease looking for*
> *flowers – there blooms a garden in your own*
> *home. While you go looking for trinkets, the*
> *treasure-house awaits you in your own being.*
> *There is no need for suffering – God is here.*

The saints and mystics share that as our
awareness grows, we start to transition from
human consciousness to divine consciousness.
We start to realize we are spiritual beings having
a human experience. The awakening of the soul
comes with this realization. As Maharaj Charan
Singh shares:

> *God is one and all souls are rays of that same*
> *sun. There is no difference between the rays*

and the sun. The rays come from the sun and merge back into the sun. So the soul comes from God and merges back into the same God. Potentially, every soul is God, because its origin is the creator.

The Beloved wants us to search for and find our origin – to experience this awakening fully during this lifetime. Why? As Hafiz shares:

We have been in love with God for so very, very long.

The mystics tell us there is no journey – we are already cupped in the essence of the Lord, we are of that essence. We just have to realize the significance of our spiritual heritage, and that is awakened through remembrance of God.

The saints say we have developed relationships for twenty, thirty or more years during our lifetime with family and friends; but the relationship with the Creator has been going on since the very start of our existence. They urge us to build a relationship with the One who has loved us from the beginning of time.

So where are our thoughts and actions leading us – toward the activities and illusions of this transitory worldly existence, or inward through contemplation on the Beloved? Hafiz says:

When the mind is consumed with remembrance of him, something divine happens to the heart that shapes the hand and tongue and eye into the word LOVE.

And it says in *The Book of Mirdad*:

Remember that the key to Life is the Creative Word. The key to the Creative Word is Love. The key to Love is Understanding. Fill up your hearts with these.
The key to Life is the Creative Word;
The key to the Creative Word is Love;
The key to Love is Understanding.

Let us begin the journey, my friends!

4

The key

The mystics tell us our souls are in the process of great transitions – turning from the outer world of illusion to the inner world – where God is fine-tuning our moments!

Hafiz has this insight to share:

The clear night sky tried to prepare me for
What it knew would someday happen;
It began to show me ever deeper aspects of
Its splendor, and then one evening just directly
Asked, 'Will you be able to withstand your
own magnificence?'
I thought I was just hearing things, until
A spring orchard I was passing my days with
At the height of its glory burst into song,
About our – every human's – destiny, to burn
With radiance.
Still I felt my ears were playing tricks on
Me until the morning came when

God tore apart my chest...
Needing more room to bloom inside...

What an incredible visual for us – God needs more room to bloom inside! The saints and mystics advise that stepping away from the ego – the I-ness that closes doors and veils the soul from the sweetness of the Friend – can open doors that allow the soul to feel and cherish the Lord's presence in each moment.

One of the keys to understanding the worth of a soul is to step aside, reflect, be open to the possibilities, to seek and experience what the Lord is offering.

The mystics and saints advise that the first important step is the willingness to change.

What does this mean? They tell us that we don't have to change professions, leave our families or let go of our religious beliefs.

Being open to change means being aware of the possibilities and opportunities that each day brings. In order to experience the depth of God's love, the saints tell us not to limit or confine ourselves to what we think we know.

The mystics and saints want us to start identifying with what is permanent and lasting – the soul. Rumi puts it this way:

A spirit that lives in this world
And does not wear the shirt of love,
Such an existence is a deep disgrace.
Be foolishly in love,
because love is all there is.
There is no way into presence
except through a love exchange.
If someone asks, But what is love?
answer, Dissolving the will.
True freedom comes to those
who have escaped the questions
of freewill and fate.
Love is an emperor.
The two worlds play across him.
He barely notices their tumbling game.
Love and lover live in eternity.
Other desires are substitutes
for that way of being.
How long do you lie embracing a corpse?
Love rather the soul, which cannot be held.
Anything born in spring dies in the fall,

but love is not seasonal.
With wine pressed from grapes,
expect a hangover.
But the love path has no expectations.
You are uneasy riding the body?
Dismount. Travel lighter.
Wings will be given.
Be clear like a mirror
reflecting nothing.
Be clean of pictures and the worry
that comes with images.
Gaze into what is not ashamed
or afraid of any truth.
Contain all human faces in your own
without any judgment of them.
Be pure emptiness.
What is inside that? you ask.
Silence is all I can say.
Lovers have some secrets
that they keep.

5

Shifting into love

Shifting into love sounds magical. But we will see it is hard work to undertake the process that will transform our habits, thinking, reactions and overall state of being. The saints and mystics tell us it does not happen overnight – it is a slow process that takes effort at each step.

Rumi tells us:

Rise up nimbly
And go on your strange journey
To the ocean of meanings.
The stream knows
It can't stay on the mountain.
Leave and don't look away
From the sun as you go,
In whose light
You're sometimes crescent,
Sometimes full.

Rumi makes several important points here. He tells us to go forward – take those steps that will allow the journey to unfold its mysteries. He goes on to say, don't look away from the sun – that light of God that knows, sees and understands our soul completely.

The mystics say that taking the steps that shift our consciousness from the outer awareness of worldly things, into an inner awareness that we are spiritual beings is essential. They tell us it is this step-by-step process that awakens us into the fullness of love. To understand the truth we need to develop our spiritual senses.

Rumi has another poignant message to share:

We always see the qualities that are living in us... Don't keep repeatedly doing what your animal-soul wants to do... Your spirit needs to follow the changes happening in the spacious place it knows about. There, the scene is always new, a clairvoyant river of picturing, more beautiful than any on earth. This is where the Sufis wash. Purify your eyes, and see the pure world. Your life will fill with radiant forms. It's a question of cleaning then developing spiritual senses! See beyond phenomena.

34

Cleansing the vessel, being willing to shift what we think we know into actual experience takes action on our part. We may ask, is the effort worth it? The mystics tell us Yes. Every step toward self-realization will help us believe, accept and trust the changes that are taking place.

Now that we can see more of the big picture, perhaps it is wise to simply look at the moments, so the journey doesn't seem overwhelming. The mystics say everything in life is accomplished step-by-step. If we take care of the moments, our spiritual senses will start to develop and we will begin to see the whole play of life unfold and our understanding will grow accordingly.

Mark Nepo has this interesting statement in his book, *The Exquisite Risk*:

> *Consider the words science and conscience. Science comes from the Latin scientia, 'to know', while conscience comes from the Latin sciens, 'to know well.' We could characterize the ability to know as retaining information and the ability to know things well as internalizing what matters.*

The mystics tell us that although we may think we know, we actually have a very limited sphere of knowledge. They say our minds are extremely limited when it comes to spirituality.

Unless we experience the truth for ourselves, within ourselves, how can we possibly know the One who is above mind and matter? The saints say this is the entire purpose of our lives – to devote ourselves to the Lord and unite with him.

Maharaj Charan Singh says:

The Lord has blessed us with the form of the human body to make it possible for us to do our real work, to apply ourselves to the activity which frees us from the constraints of the physical body, so that we can merge with Him.

Let us now talk about who the mystics call the Friend – and dive into their advice!

6

Meeting the friend

Many of us have been seeking for a long time. Perhaps we find ourselves restless, dissatisfied with the world and asking questions about the true purpose of this human life. We may read volumes and go to places of worship to find truth, but we come away unfulfilled and still hungry to know 'why'.

We may have had a shock or death of a loved one show us how temporary this life is. So we keep asking why are we here and what do we need to know? Maharaj Charan Singh tells us:

To be in the human body is like being a resident of a very beautiful town where it is possible to purchase the supreme bargain of God. It is only while we are human that we are capable of obtaining this bargain of devotion and love for Him and the longing to merge with Him. This is why Masters instruct us to keep our aim and objective clearly before our eyes, so that we may take maximum advantage of such an opportunity.

If we are to achieve our goal and fulfil the supreme purpose of human life, then we must search for our destination, and make progress on our spiritual journey while we are living in the body.

The saints and mystics tell us that we will be able to discover what is real in the appearances, objects and relationships of this world when we find a teacher who has walked this road and experienced the inner path.

They say we will begin to understand the law of karma (As you sow, so shall you reap), which underlies and encompasses everything in life. Most importantly, they tell us we will begin to understand the relationship between the soul and the supreme Lord.

The saints provide us now with some of the answers to our questions of who we are and why we need a spiritual guide – the Friend – and what will happen when we follow his/her instructions.

The mystics tell us the soul is a particle of the supreme Lord, a drop of the ocean of his love. They explain that we will find God's love through the Word, Logos, Shabd or Holy Spirit.

Our teacher can help us find a practice that will immerse us into God's Word, the holy Name, and through dedicated effort and the Lord's grace, the soul will ultimately be reunited with its source.

The mystics explain in detail how the spiritual journey starts from the soles of the feet and reaches up to the crown of the head. There are two stages in this journey, they tell us. The first reaches up to the eyes, and the second is above the eyes.

Within the body, the seat of the mind and soul is behind the eyes, and this is the same for everyone. You may have heard this point between the eyes called the window, the tenth door or the gateway. This tenth door opens inward.

By practicing the techniques explained to us by the mystics and saints, we withdraw our scattered attention and retrace its outward flow, so that it becomes focused at this point behind the eyes, at the tenth door.

Once our mind calms down and stays steady at this inner focal point, we will automatically develop inner consciousness and begin to hear a sweet and most melodious sound, or call, which emanates from the court of the Lord.

Maharaj Charan Singh shares:

*This Call is present in everyone – in thieves,
thugs, holy men, saints and enlightened
beings – irrespective of community, religion
or nation. Hindu, Sikh or Christian – one's
religion makes no difference, providing one
can go within oneself. Anyone who is blessed
with the great good fortune of being able to
focus his attention, his soul current, at the
eye center, will begin to hear the melodious
resonance of the Word ringing within himself
and will begin to see its light and brilliance.
With the help of this Audible Sound, the Call,
the Logos, he is able to establish the direction
of his home within, and guided by its light, he
is able to travel on his spiritual journey.*

We may ask 'How can I meet the Friend, the
well-wisher, the teacher and guide who can show
me the way?'

Remember that famous song that contained the
lyrics 'Seek and ye shall find, knock and the door
shall be opened, ask and it shall be given...'? The
saints and mystics tell us that every moment we
seek to know the Lord, sincerely ask to find Him
and knock on his door, the Lord's grace will guide
us to the right path to continue the journey.

John Ortberg, in his book, *God Is Closer than You Think*, has this insight:

God wants to be known, but not in a way that overwhelms us, that takes away the possibility of love freely chosen.

This is what we need to remember at the onset: spending the day with God does not usually involve doing different things from what we already do. Mostly it involves learning to do what we already do in a new way – with God.

Each one of us has been called – summoned by the Beloved. The mystics tell us that everyone has within himself the capacity to realize the Lord while in this human body. In *Perfume of the Desert*, Andrew Harvey tells us:

Perhaps only a small handful will do what the true seeker does when love's call is heard – reorganize his or her whole life to try to absorb more and more of what love is saying... This is the journey to God... You have to take the summons seriously, recognize its sacred demand on you to transform your life and being, and turn your heart wholly toward the Beloved.

If we earnestly seek, the saints and mystics tell us that the Friend, the well-wisher, the one who can help guide us on this incredible journey, will definitely come into our lives.

Through his/her own experience, the Friend will help us transition from worldly beings into spiritual beings – and will never leave us. The mystics say that our Friend will always be there to offer support and advice on how to walk the path to God-realization.

Shaikh Abu-Saeed Abil-Kheir shares this message:

When the desire for the Friend became real,
All existence fell behind.
The Beloved wasn't interested in my reasoning.
I threw it away and became silent.
The sanity I had been taught became a bore,
It had to be ushered off.
Insane, silent and in bliss,
I spent my days with my head
At the feet of my Beloved.

So what next? Into the Depth of Love we go!

7

The heart of love

From the *Treasury of Mystic Terms* comes this quote:

Mystics say that the nature of God is love, that he is an ocean of love. The experience of this love is deeply blissful and entrancing, and once a soul gets a taste of it, all other pleasures pale by comparison. They automatically detach the mind from the world and from the creation. Love and bliss are primary attributes of the soul, as well as of God, and the closer a soul becomes to Him, the more is divine bliss experienced.

The mystics tell us that love is the core of our being. It is fuel to the fire of life and the very essence of existence. But how do we attain love?

The mystics say the mind is one of the biggest obstacles to understanding our true spiritual nature. Love cannot be purchased, knowledge cannot contain it, and words cannot bind it. Simply stated – logic and love do not mix.

This is where transitions come in. In order to grow spiritually, the saints say we have to give up our cleverness and ideas on how to achieve love. We have to go beyond reasoning and analyzing and open the gateway to the heart.

What do the saints suggest? Look within, follow the path of the Friend. Rumi tells us to say to the mind:

> Dear mind, such a traveler, always moving,
> like a fish looking for the sea, while the great
> heart's ocean waits all around and inside it.
> How can you live outside this love?

Actually, saints and mystics tell us that we can't live outside this love. That is why we feel the longing, the pull, the restlessness deep inside our being.

Without experiencing divine love, we are simply an empty shell acting on the stage of life. If love is the core of our being as the mystics teach, then it is necessary to seek the source of this love and dive into this love to become truly alive.

We will never be complete or whole until we experience this divine love in every pore of our being. The mystics encourage us when they say it is possible to achieve the goal of God-realization now – right now – while we have the gift of the human body.

This is the soul's destiny. To experience the Lord's divine love is our spiritual heritage. This is why the saints talk of the importance of seeking divine love with every breath that we take.

In the Bible Christ tells us, 'If thine eye be single, thy whole body shall be full of light.' The mystics tell us that our soul is composed of light and sound, not these outer physical attributes, blood and bones that we are so attached to.

The physical is subject to change, to decay and death, but not the soul. The saints say the soul is eternal, deathless and everlasting. There is no better time than right now to open the heart to love, nourish the soul and find the joy that lies within.

The saints and mystics talk about the heart of love – what it is and how we find it. Maharaj Sawan Singh tells us:

> *Love is the richest of all treasures.*
> *Without it there is nothing, and with it*
> *there is everything.*

The world is beautiful and we are naturally attracted towards it, because the Creator of both man and the world is the same God, who is Love.

God has filled both man and the world with currents of love, and the world is supported by love. Love's magnetic power is at work throughout the entire world. The sun, moon, earth, stars, sky – all are sending out currents of love to others.

We all have a natural attraction to the world that the Lord has created, but there is even a stronger pull, the mystics tell us, toward the Creator – the source of love.

This pull, longing or motivation is a driving force within that opens the heart and expands the awareness. It is like a river that is drawing water from the hill and mountain streams to swell and grow until it reaches its source, the ocean.

The saints teach that love is a beautiful and sublime experience of the heart. Maharaj Sawan Singh tells us:

A place where there is love becomes sanctified by it. If we perform our domestic and other worldly duties with love, we shall enjoy our life in comfort and without any

worries, because in the presence of love, the
mind and intellect are powerless to disturb
one's inner calmness. Love does not influence
only human beings. Even the animals and
birds are subject to its elevating influence.

The mystics don't tell us to leave our families or worldly work; instead they say do everything with love, and start feeling the deep inner happiness and contentment that stems from that love. With love as the base we become better human beings in thought, word and deed.

The saints say that God looks on all beings as the same, and they ask us to love one another, as the light of God shines in everyone.

When Saint John was asked to address a gathering of children, what did he say? 'Little children, love one another.' He repeated this three times and when asked if he hadn't anything of more importance to say, he replied:

I give this advice over and over again, because
of all the qualities, that of love is the greatest
need of mankind. If you would love each other
and the current of love would fill your minds,
you would possess all other good qualities.
Love, and all things shall be added unto you.

The mystics and saints tell us that love is the beauty of the soul and that it is not possible to describe the sweetness of love's qualities.

They tell us that love is the soul's true nature – its divine birthright. Maharaj Sawan Singh says:

> The meaning of Prem (love) is the merging of one's self into the object of love. It has a wonderful attraction or strong pulling power. The word 'prem' is derived from the Sanskrit word 'pre', which means a thing that pleases the heart and attracts it. Another definition of 'prem' is surrender of the heart.

Love is that which transforms the small drop of the soul into the ocean of God.

I remember attending a meeting one evening, and the speaker gave this great visual about love. The story was about an elderly poet near the end of his life. It was about the hourglass – how each grain of sand was related to the self and the ego, our attachments and desires. And as each grain fell through the small opening towards the bottom of the hourglass, love grew in a slow but ever bigger pile.

Now at the end of his life most of the sand was at the bottom of the hourglass and that made him full of love – all the other elements of life had slowly sifted away with the passage of time. All that was left was love!

Guru Arjan has described this state:

The rays have merged in the sun, the drops into the sea; light has merged into the Supreme Light, and I am fulfilled.

8

Patience, perseverance and practice

We all know that nothing is achieved without effort. We set goals, and work to achieve those goals throughout our lives. Inner work takes patience, perseverance and practice every step of the way.

In Persian, the word *sabr* means patience, resilience and endurance. The Sufi mystics frequently refer to this concept.

We need patience because we don't know and understand the inner path fully as yet – each moment we are learning new things, and our teacher is showing us what to expect along the way. With patience comes trust, and trust develops a willingness to take the steps necessary to achieve God-realization.

There is a popular story by Tibetan teachers:

A hermit was living alone in the mountains. One day, a herdsman happened to pass his cave. Intrigued, the herdsman shouted at the hermit and asked, 'What are you doing alone in the middle of nowhere?' The hermit replied, 'I am meditating.'

'What are you meditating on?' asked the herdsman. 'On patience,' said the hermit.

Several authors have given us some insights into patience. There are many different perspectives to choose from, but patience is so fruitful – anger is dispelled, tolerance and forbearance are cultivated and we appreciate each moment for what it offers.

Leo Tolstoy tells us:

The two most powerful warriors are patience and time.

M.J. Ryan in her book, *The Power of Patience,* shares:

If we want to live wider and deeper lives, not just faster ones, we have to practice patience.

Scott Curran tells us:

When you encounter various trials, big or small, be full of joy. They're opportunities to learn patience.

Perseverance means taking action and continuing with our practice, so we achieve what we are seeking. A daily routine really helps establish the habit of stilling both body and mind, allowing us to let go of preconceived ideas and become receptive to what lies within.

Two dictionary definitions define perseverance in this way:

Perseverance – sometimes called 'grit' – is the great leveler.

Steady persistence in a course of action, a purpose, a state… especially in spite of difficulty, obstacles or discouragement.

The mystics always tell us to be consistent in our meditation and remembrance of the Lord. By doing so, we keep the mind focused on the goal and stay more balanced throughout life's ups and downs.

In *Spiritual Perspectives* Maharaj Charan Singh answers a question about effort and the Lord's grace:

Brother, it takes both. We have to put in the effort, and the grace of the Master (the Lord) is always there. My Master used to tell us that if a disciple goes one step forward, the Master comes ten steps to receive him. If we go ten steps, he comes a hundred steps to receive us. If we are sincere and honest in our devotion, in our efforts, he never withholds his grace. It is always there.... So even our one step is sufficient for him to pull us.

Every little effort counts in the court of the Lord.

Tao Te Ching reminds us that the journey of a thousand miles begins with a single step!

Practice makes perfect. Step by step as we walk the path with our teacher and guide, our friend and well-wisher, we will find that the more effort we make, the more grace will be there to help us make even more effort. It is a wonderful circle of love.

Bhai Gurdas tells us:

If you take one step to take refuge in the Master,
The Master meets you on the way
By taking hundreds of steps.

If you remember the Master just once,
The Master remembers you again and again.
Even if your devotion is as small
As a fragment of a cowrie shell,
The Master showers all benefits on you.
The Master is all merciful.
His praise is beyond understanding.
I bow again and again
To the one and incomprehensible Master.

The mystics and saints tell us that through practice and perseverance we become receptive to the Lord's love.

Maharaj Charan Singh continues speaking about grace, saying:

God's grace is always there, brother, but we
have to become receptive to his grace. If it is
raining very heavily and your cup is upside
down, not a drop of water will get into it. You
have to put the cup with the right side up, and
then it will be filled with rain water. God's
grace is always there, within every one of us,
but we have to withdraw our consciousness
to that point where his grace is coming day
and night. Unless we attach ourselves to that

and unless we are filled with that love and devotion for the Lord, naturally these desires and attachments of the world will not go out of us. There is no limit to his grace, which is everywhere, but we have to be receptive.

Hafiz puts it like this:

I confided in the wind all my fond hopes.
Trust in God's grace, the wind replied.
The evening supplication, the morning prayer,
Are the keys to the treasure you are searching for.
Go forth this way and the road will lead you
To the one who is the keeper of your heart.

9

True devotion

The saints tell us that devotion is a quality by which the soul rises upwards and attains communion with God. Through practice of the Word, God's Name, and following the instructions of our teacher, the attention is slowly removed from the outward objects of the world and starts to focus on the Lord.

Maulana Rum says:

We should sit at the feet of a person who knows our hearts, who can understand our difficulties and sufferings, who can share our sadness and who can remove it. We should sit in the shade of a tree bearing fresh flowers and fruit, which will refresh our mind and heart, and from which we will get the fruit of spiritual life to eat.... We should sit someplace where we can have the Lord's nectar.

Most of us have some idea of what devotion is. We might be devoted to our family, friends, pets – even our car! But when the saints and mystics talk about devotion, they are talking about a devotion that fills the spiritual heart with longing and love for the Lord. They tell us that love is a flame that, when kindled, burns everything away – only God remains.

Maharaj Sawan Singh tells us:

> *Devotion is a spontaneous magnetic current which attracts one towards one's Beloved. It is not a subject for reasoning or even for thinking. It is an intuitive emotion of love. Devotion is a natural attribute of the heart.*

How do we grow in devotion for the Lord? The mystics say we can come to know the Lord intimately by embracing His Word, Bani, Name, Shabd, the Nam.

The mystics ask us to switch our devotion from objects and faces of the world and develop love for His Name – the Word of God, which is the source of all life.

Devotion can be found in our everyday existence, if our focus remains on seeking the source. God knows and loves everyone equally, so everyone can attain union with Him.

Eknath has a wonderful poem called "Carefree":

If you embrace his Name with love,
All your worries will be his.
Feel sad about nothing –
God knows and cares for everyone.
Never would he desert you.
Whatever your state, let it be.
See the wonder
Of your ancient debts dissolved.
By his grace, the harvest of your actions
Scheduled for this very life
Will be destroyed, says Eknath.

There are some important messages for us in Eknath's poem. He tells us to 'embrace his Name with love'. How do we accomplish this? The mystics tell us that the longing and love will grow with attention – turning inward toward the Lord, and focusing on repeating his Name.

This will drive out all 'otherness' and we will feel closer to the One who truly loves us. His presence will be our constant companion, if we but repeat his Name sincerely.

The mystics assure us devotion will build, longing will grow and we will be immersed in his love if we put in the effort.

Samarth Ramdas shares:

Ceaselessly repeat the Name of God
And you'll find fulfillment.
Every day, and regularly –
Early morning, afternoon and evening –
Keep repeating the Name.
Through times of happiness or hardship,
Times auspicious or inauspicious,
Resting and sleeping, keep repeating the Name.
Walking, talking, eating, working,
Enjoying the pleasures of life,
Never forget the Name.
Rich or poor – whatever your destiny –
Stay in the atmosphere of the Name.
In childhood and youth, in dark days and old age,
In all stages of life – and at the end –
Keep repeating the Name.
The Name destroys mountains of misdeeds,
And it's open to everyone – it knows no
High or low, intelligent or dull.
All can cross the ocean of existence.

In the above lines, Samarth Ramdas is telling us that we can go through everyday life as usual, just bring the Name of God into our thoughts, and through that remembrance devotion will be cultivated. He goes on in this poem:

You are the comfort of my soul
In the seasons of sorrow.
You are the wealth of my spirit
In the heartbreak of loss.
The unimaginable,
The unknowable –
That is what you give my soul
When it moves in your direction.
By your grace
My eyes have looked upon eternity.

This state is the ultimate for the seeker after truth. The mystics tell us that to understand and identify with the soul is to unlock the gateway to eternity. Ramdas continues:

O King, how could this crumbling empire
Ever take me from you?
The voice that sings your name
Is sweeter than midnight sleep,

More graceful than the song of a royal poet.
When deep in prayer
My faith is bound by the thought of You.

Ramdas here speaks of the world – the crumbling empire. The saints tell us that everything in this world is impermanent and transitory – subject to change – thus slowly crumbling around us. The real wealth lies within, and it is lasting, permanent, unchanging. Ramdas goes on to explain:

You melt stone hearts with love.
If I were offered a kingdom,
And the world's riches were placed at my feet,
I would bow with my face low and say,
This does not compare to His love!
Union is the pure wine.
My life is the cup.
Without your wine
What use is this cup?

The true meaning of life, the mystics say, is to embrace God's love, to find that union which is permanent and lasting in these shifting sands of time and space.

This love and devotion will grow and grow within the soul, and ultimately this rich feeling of being immersed in the Lord's love is all that we will long for throughout our days.

Devotion is an essential and important part of spirituality, as we see in the following lines of Ramdas:

I once had a thousand desires,
But in my one desire to know You
All else melted away.
The pure essence of Your being
Has taken over my heart and soul.
Through your grace I have found
A treasure within myself.
I have found the truth of the unseen world.
I have gone beyond the ravages of time.
I have become one with You!

This then is the essence the saints share – union with the beloved Lord. With attention and focus, effort and grace, the final merging will take place. Ramdas concludes:

Now my heart sings....
From my first breath I have longed for Him –
This longing has become my life.

The mystics explain that if we immerse ourselves in devotion for the Lord, we will go back to our true eternal home. We will begin to realize that this human form is bestowed upon us for the sole purpose of attaining God-realization. We may seek and put in the effort, but the saints also tell us that the gift of true devotion is in the hands of God.

Maharaj Sawan Singh explains:

He Himself makes it possible for us to be His devotees. He cuts asunder all the ties binding His devotees to the world and makes them free. It is only by the grace of the Lord that it is possible for human beings to perceive God.

The saints tell us that the Lord loves our efforts, and true devotion will blossom if we simply continue to try.

The practice of the Word is what the mystics call true devotion. It is because of this practice that we are able to join ourselves with the truth, and the Name of God is imprinted in our minds permanently.

Saints and mystics describe the Name or Word of God as a very rare thing. From *Kabir, the Weaver of God's Name*:

Kabir says that he has found it, and it is
priceless, indivisible and indestructible.
Shabd, the Word, the Name of God, Nam, the
sound current, the divine melody or nectar,
pervades the entire creation. it is beyond the
reach of scholarship and intellect, yet dwells
within every human being. Kabir says:

I have found something,
Something rare I have found;
Its value none can assess.
It has no color, it is one,
Indivisible and everlasting...
Untouched by the waves of change,
It fills each and every vessel.
It has no weight, it has no price;
Beyond the bounds of measurement,
It cannot be counted,
And through erudition
It cannot be known.
It is neither heavy nor light.
No touchstone can assay its worth.
I dwell in it, it dwells in me,
We are one, like water
Mixed with water.
Kabir, the Lord's slave, has discovered

An ocean filled with the nectar of love,
But I find no one disposed to taste it.
When men do not believe my words,
Words from my own experience,
What else can I say to convince them?

What happens in our minds when the soul merges into God's Truth? Kabir says we discover 'an ocean filled with the nectar of love.' This is our real wealth, and can only be gathered while in this human body.

Maharaj Charan Singh puts it this way:

While we are alive we should gather what is
our own here and will remain ours hereafter.
This wealth is devotion to Nam, attaching the
mind and the soul currents to the Audible Life
Stream, the Word or Logos.

The mystics remind us that God is love and everyone is entitled to enter the path of devotion. One who tastes the fruit of devotion will be fully satisfied.

Now comes the effort – walking the path to attain liberation of the soul.

Spiritual transitions require shifting from the outer world of phenomena to the inner world of God-realization. It takes a great deal of time and effort to refocus our priorities to reflect our intentions. That is why setting a goal is an invaluable tool on this journey to God.

10

Setting the goal

The walkways of our lives are paved with good intentions. We make promises to ourselves, yet time and life seem to slip by at an alarming rate, until one day we realize we haven't achieved what we had hoped for in terms of realizing God.

The mystics advise us to set a goal for ourselves. This is a personal decision for each soul. Once we understand what is the most important aim in this life we have been blessed with, they tell us to put blinders on and go forward with courage and determination, and the Lord's grace will be there to help us every step of the way.

None of us is perfect – we make mistakes and slip and fall away from our goals – but we can get back on track. Remember the story of the Prodigal Son? Here is a version told by John Leeming:

Many years ago, a young man
Grew up in a small town.
The house was old and the yard

Backed on the railroad tracks.
Life was not easy, there were
Times of hunger and times of cold;
But there was love and understanding
And faith in God.
In his late teens he became restive,
As most teenagers do.
He challenged the authority at home,
At school; challenged the rules of society.
When parents, school and society
Would not yield, he lashed out.
Finally, after much bitterness, he left home,
And his parents could not stop him.

This is part of the restlessness the saints talk about – the restlessness of the soul wanting to find its true home. But this young man still had quite a journey of discovery in front of him, just as all of us do!

The world is tempting, but not kind.
The young man slipped to a low path.
Many things he did to hurt others
And to hurt himself.
He lost touch with his parents,
As he feared to tell them what he did.

He travelled far and he travelled light,
Feeling no homeward pull.
After many years, many empty years,
Sharp edges and appetites are dulled.
What satisfied yesterday does not today;
And change produces only change.
Attachments have not turned to love;
Loneliness is his only constant companion.
Free, yes, from obedience to a guiding hand,
But such a heavy price to pay!

Most of us can probably identify with this young man. Full of ideals and righteousness, he thinks he can conquer life on his own terms in his own way, not having to listen to others tell him what is best. Eventually, however, he finds life is an empty shell, with loneliness his bedfellow and no love to support him.

As another year drew toward its end
With short, cold days and leaden skies,
The songs, the lights, the cheer of
Coming Christmas caught his ear and eye;
Stirred soft and long forgotten feelings
Deep within; lighted again his soul.
And memories of the warmth of love, of home,
Overpowered old hurts and fears.

The saints share that deep inside all of us is the desire to know God – a hunger for the truth: the soul is missing warmth, love and its real home.

Hesitating, often with hope crushed
By fear of deeper loss, he planned,
Then wrote; 'Dad, Mom,
May I come home for Christmas?
Will you take me in again,
Forgiving what was said and done?
Till now I did not know how dear the loss,
How deep my need for you.

What courage it took to write that letter and take the following steps! He did not know whether he would be welcome or shut away from all he held dear.

'Dad, time is short, too short
To have your answer, yes or no.
So I will start, and as a sign
If I am welcome home,
Hang a white cloth in the old
Apple tree in the back yard.
I will see it from the train,
But pass on by if it be not there.'

So we start seeking and taking those steps to see that if we make the effort, the Lord will welcome us home. Our hearts are open and vulnerable as we reach out for those answers. But are we willing to take the chance?

Some days later, huddled in a coach seat,
Pride and arrogance of youth
Honed by life to humility and need,
Hope alone remained.
He could not bring himself to look
Upon that backyard tree.
He lacked the strength of faith
To see what fate would bring.

What we really want to know is what our destiny will bring – but we start to realize that nothing is in our hands, and we open ourselves to the grace of the Giver, the one who loves us completely.

And so, he turned to one nearby,
Saying, 'Friend, around the next curve
We will pass a small house,
In the backyard is an old apple tree.
Please watch and tell me
If you see a small white cloth

Hanging on a branch of the tree
As a sign if I am welcome home.'
'Certainly, son', was the reply. 'I will
Look and tell you what I see.'

Can you imagine how anxious this young man was in these moments? Not knowing whether he would be welcome or not? Not knowing whether he would ever again share his father's love?

Around the curve, and his companion
Cried, 'Look, look you must!
Every branch, no every twig,
Hung with banners shining white.
Surely you are welcome home,
So welcome home!'

The Lord cherishes every soul – He will never let us down – his love is unchanging through these shifting sands of time and space.

Thus too, with each of us
Who will turn again to Home;
Who asks, with humility and hope,
'Father, will you take me back?'
Faint hope is soon replaced with faith

As in His everlasting Love
The answer rings with sound and light,
'Oh welcome, welcome home!'

This is the goal that the mystics tell us is within reach, my friends – the Lord is anxiously waiting to welcome us home!

11

Walking the talk

What part of 'us' is real and lasting, we might ask. We all have the desire to know and comprehend who we really are – spiritual beings having this human experience. We make plans to understand what this means, and have the very best of intentions to follow the instructions of our teacher, friend and well-wisher who has offered to guide us on the Path that we have chosen.

Then why does it appear to be so difficult to actually 'walk the talk'? Hafiz tells us:

What is the difference
Between your experience of Existence
And that of a saint?
The saint knows
That the spiritual path
Is a sublime chess game with God
And that the Beloved
Has just made such a Fantastic Move

That the saint is now continually
Tripping over Joy
And bursting out in Laughter
And saying, 'I surrender!'
Whereas, my dear,
I am afraid you still think
You have a thousand serious moves.

Wow – when we hear what Hafiz is telling us, that we still think we have a thousand serious moves to make in this chess game of life, the inner secret starts to unveil itself – do we really have choices?

Epictetus says:

Happiness and freedom begin with a clear understanding of one principle: some things are within our control, and some things are not.

The saints and mystics all tell us that to truly understand our spiritual nature, we need to put in the effort, follow the precepts of our teacher and guide, and take responsibility for our choices and actions.

The mystics continue, saying we have limited choice. Our destiny will bring us into a certain situation, and how we react to that situation will either bind us further to this creation or help us burn through the layer of karma and lighten our load.

Let's take an example: If we were to walk up to the top of a twelve-story building and go out on the roof, we would have a choice to make – do we jump off or do we turn around and go back down the stairs.

Whatever choice we make, we need to take responsibility for our actions. One is a positive choice and one is a negative choice. The negative choice could create a new chain of karma, while the positive choice may erase old karmic patterns.

The saints and mystics talk a lot about karma – what does this word mean and how does it affect us? Basically, they tell us that karma is the law of action and reaction – we harvest the fruit or result of past thoughts, words and deeds.

Indian mystics say we have three types of karma:

Pralabdh karma, which is also called fate or destiny, and is allotted to us in this birth.

Kriyaman karma, which is the result or fruit of new actions performed during the present birth.

Sinchit karma, or those karmas that still remain to be taken out of our own stored-up reservoir and are to be worked out in future incarnations.

The Bible says – As you sow, so shall you reap. The mystics remind us that every action, every choice we make, becomes our responsibility – and we can either create or reduce our karmic load accordingly.

In this poignant poem by Rumi, we see what lies ahead:

Strive, struggle, grapple and wrestle,
None won the battle by weak-kneed submission.
Go on scratching, scraping and cutting
The stone wall that bars your way.
Cut, hew, gash, break, shatter, demolish, smash:
Rest not for a second, till your very last breath arrives.
Even a worthless effort is better than sleeping,
For the Lord loves our effort, anxiety and struggle.
First put in full effort, then accept what he sends.
Have faith in him and trust his will....
March on until you reach his gate.
When the Master has put a sword in your hands,
He has clearly expressed his wish.

This is the inner secret! The friend, teacher, guide or mystic has put a sword into our hands. They know the path for they have walked it in its entirety and can show us the way back to God. It takes trust, patience, effort and grace, but the saints and mystics explain that it is possible to realize God now, while in this human body.

Brother Lawrence tells us what our attitude should be on this journey to God:

We should not be seeking consolation from this practice, but let us do it motivated by love and because God wishes it.

Brother Lawrence goes on to encourage us by saying:

There is no mode of life in the world more pleasing and more full of delight than continual conversation with God; only those who practice and experience it can understand it.

Here Brother Lawrence gives us encouragement to practice and experience God's continual presence in our lives. The mystics say it will take effort and more effort on our part, but the end result will be what the soul is seeking – union with the Beloved.

Brother Lawrence shares a deep insight when he says:

In the beginning, we have to make an effort to renounce ourselves, but after that there is no longer anything but unutterable contentment. When we face difficulties, we have only to run back to the Lord and ask Him for His grace. When He grants it, everything becomes easy.

It is a common thing to just be content to do penances and private spiritual exercises, forgetting about love which is the end and purpose of it all. It is easy to recognize this by the works that such things produce and that is why so little concrete spiritual virtue can be found.

It is not necessary to have either a keen intellect or great knowledge to go to God, but simply a heart resolved to apply itself to Him and for Him, and to love only Him.

12

Honest effort

Step by step we fine tune our lives so we can appreciate and practice what our teacher advises us to do. The mystics and saints tell us that we need to be scrupulously honest with ourselves to make headway on the spiritual path. What does this mean?

They say being a good human being, developing compassion, kindness and helpfulness coupled with a non-judgmental attitude will help us walk the path we have chosen.

Leading a moral and upright life and attending to our devotion for as much time as possible keeps us balanced and focused on the goal – God-realization.

The mystics and saints say our devotion needs to take on a practical form, reflecting in every daily action and in our whole routine. This will build an atmosphere that keeps us turning inward, helping us to become more and more aware of God's presence in our lives. Our whole life becomes a wonderful circle of love!

Baba Kuhi of Shiraz shares the ultimate realization for a seeker – the more we practice, the more we realize that only God exists.

In the marketplace, in the monastery, I saw only God.

In the valley, on the mountaintop, I saw only God.

In the darkness of ordeal, I saw Him bright beside me.

In good luck or tragedy, I saw only God.

In prayer, in fasting, in celebration, in contemplation,

In all the glory of the Prophet's religion,

I saw only God.

I did not see 'soul' or 'body', 'accident' or 'substance.'

I did not see 'attributes' or 'causes', I saw only God.

I opened wide my eyes and by the blaze of His Face

Everything was lit with vision, and I saw only God.

In the fire of His ecstasy I melted like a candle;

His flames rushed at me from all sides, and I saw only God.

When I looked with my own eyes, I saw only myself.

When I came to look with God's eyes, I saw only God.

I was annihilated by Love and vanished into Nowhere –

Suddenly I was the All-Living One, and saw only God.

This is so beautiful, as it describes the state of union with the Beloved, where only He exists. He becomes the center of our life.

The mystics say as we walk along this path, we start to see the Lord everywhere and in everything, and the heart softens and expands to encompass appreciation for the whole of the Lord's creation. These are magic moments in life – to lose the self and merge into the One who loves us completely. What a gift!

In the Bhagavad Gita we read:

> *Constantly mastering his mind,*
> *The spiritual man grows peaceful,*
> *Attains supreme bliss,*
> *And returns to the Absolute One.*

The saints tell us that as we follow the path, our perspective on life changes and we start to see more and more clearly what our true purpose is. We start to rise above and break free from limitations that may be blocking the inner way.

Hector Esponda Dubin tells us in *Living Meditation*:

To follow the path to its destination means
nothing less than the journey of a lifetime.
As we travel along it and our mind becomes
steadier through the practice of meditation
(prayer and devotion), we will experience the
soul gaining control while the undisciplined
and ever-troublesome aspects of our mind
are progressively weakened. Life becomes
more carefree...and we find ourselves more
balanced and content.

Wouldn't we all like to be more balanced and content? The mystics share that the more we turn our attention inward, this balance and contentment will grow and an indescribable joy will enter our moments. Is the effort worth it? Yes!

In *The Gospel According to Matthew* we read:

Seek ye first the kingdom of God
And everything else shall be added unto you.

There is a transformation taking place inside us. It will stun us at times as the soul starts to realize the truth and yet can be uncomfortable as changes redefine our existence.

There is a big difference between knowing the path and walking it. Nasruddin once addressed a large crowd and shouted:

'Do you want knowledge without ordeal, truth without lies, attainment without any hard work, and progress without sacrifice?'
Everyone yelled 'Yes!'

"Marvelous!' said Nasruddin. 'I do also, and if I ever find out how to manage it, I'll be thrilled to let you know.'

In this ever-changing shadow show called life, effort and persistence matter. Garth Brooks, in his 1992 song "The River," talks about making an honest effort and going with the flow:

You know a dream is like a river
Ever changin' as it flows
And a dreamer's just a vessel
That must follow where it goes.
Trying to learn from what's behind you
And never knowing what's in store
Makes each day a constant battle
Just to stay between the shores.

And I will sail my vessel
'Til the river runs dry
Like a bird upon the wind
These waters are my sky.

I'll never reach my destination
If I never try,

So I will sail my vessel
'Til the river runs dry.
Too many times we stand aside
And let the waters slip away
'Til what we put off 'til tomorrow
It has now become today.

So don't you sit upon the shoreline
And say you're satisfied,
Choose to chance the rapids
And dare to dance the tides.
And I will sail my vessel
'Til the river runs dry.
Like a bird upon the wind
These waters are my sky.
I'll never reach my destination
If I never try.

So I will sail my vessel
'Til the river runs dry.
There's bound to be rough waters
And I know I'll take some falls,

With the good Lord as my captain
I can make it through them all.
And I will sail my vessel
'Til the river runs dry.

Like a bird upon the wind
These waters are my sky.
I'll never reach my destination
If I never try
So I will sail my vessel
'Til the river runs dry.
Lord, I will sail my vessel
'Til the river runs dry.

We can all relate to the waters of life being rough at times, and we are bound to make mistakes and head in the wrong direction. But as the mystics teach, if we keep the Lord as our captain, we can weather even the most difficult of circumstances.

We can't stand aside and let life pass us by, or we will never be satisfied or reach our goal of God-realization. Effort brings the grace to put in even more effort, and we start to realize that the Beloved is always by our side, encouraging us to continue in our quest for the truth.

This is a wonderful feeling, for knowing that the Lord is always present in our life brings a sense of companionship that the world does not offer. He gives the heart the strength, support and courage to open love's doorway.

13

Love gives the soul wings

The mystics tell us there is really no mystery to the search for God – God is love and the way back to him is through love.

Richard Rolle, a fourteenth-century theologian, shares this insight:

> *If you would stand well with God, and have grace to rule your life and come to the joy of love, repeat His Name – so fasten it in your heart that it is never lost from your thought. And when you speak to Him, it shall be in your ear joy, in your mouth honey and in your heart melody... If you think of the Name continually, and hold it firmly, it purges your sin and kindles your heart. Think it (the Name) in your heart night and day as your special, dear treasure. Love it more than life, root it in your mind. Love Him for He made you. Give your heart to Him for it is in His debt. Therefore, set your love on His Name, which is healing.*

When we start to become aware, the Lord's love becomes a real and vital presence in our lives and the soul starts to awaken. The saints tell us as we focus on the Word, we will start to realize our true essence as spiritual beings. The river of the Word will give the soul wings to fly back to that One Lord who loves the soul completely.

This Word of God is not a human word, one that can be spoken and written; the mystics call it the voice of God, the audible life stream, that inner sound that opens our hearts to God .

What is this Word, also called Shabd, Nam, the Audible Life Stream, the Way? The mystics tell us this Word is the creative power that has created and sustains the entire creation and is actually the essence of the Lord. In *John* 1:1 we read:

In the beginning was the Word and the Word was with God, and the Word was God.

We'll explore the Word in greater detail in the next chapter, as it is truly love in action!

The mystics and saints tell us that as we seek to find the treasure within, the soul will begin to realize that it is part of the Whole that is God.

Hafiz shares:

(The soul) becomes so free
In a wonderful, secret
And pure love
That flows
From a conscious
One-pointed
Infinite need for Light.
Even then, my dear,
The Beloved will have fulfilled
Just a fraction
Just a fraction!
Of a promise
He wrote upon your heart.
When your soul begins
To even bloom and laugh
And spin in Eternal Ecstasy –
O little by little
You will turn into God.

The mystics tell us that it is the nature of love to melt the heart and transform the lover into the Beloved. As we walk on the path leading to the Lord, the longing will build, creating a desire to intimately know Him. The saints say we are not separate from the Beloved – can the ray ever remain separate from the sun? Our ego builds the windows and walls that keep us at a distance from what we are seeking. The Lord unlocks the doors and windows of our hearts so that we can feel His love pulsing through our every breath.

Richard Rolle expresses it beautifully:

No one can untie the knot
By which I bind your love to me
Sweet Master.
I am seeking the treasure
I long for,
But all I can find is longing,
Because I never stop thirsting for you!
Yet like the wind my sorrow
Vanishes,
For my reward is this melody
Inaudible to the human ear.
My inner being is turned
Into a song wonderfully sweet
And because of the love
I want to die.
Whenever this occurs,
And these things

Take hold of me and refresh me,
Then the size of your gifts dazzles
And delights me,
And love's approach tortures me with joy.

We may sometimes wonder, what am I here for? One answer might be 'To awaken to and experience the complete joy of His love.'

Rumi shares:

Unfold your own myth, without complicated explanation, so everyone will understand the passage 'we have opened you.' Start walking toward Shams [Rumi's spiritual teacher]. Your legs will feel heavy and tired. Then comes a moment of feeling, the wings you've grown, lifting.

14

Truth is simple

The saints and mystics tell us that Truth cannot change – perspectives may change and ideas may change, but Truth doesn't change. For all of us seeking the Truth, the spiritual essence of the soul, we need to dive into the Word.

The Word is beautifully described in *Spiritual Discourses,* volume 2:

> *Known in the different religions under a multitude of names, it designates the dynamic power of God, which created, enlivens and sustains the universe, and through which the soul returns to its source. It is the central reality of the teachings of the saints.*

Guru Arjun Dev says:

> *He who cherishes the Word within his heart, the greatest king is he; he who has Nam within his heart will fulfil the purpose of his life.*

Truth is simple – 'He who cherishes the Word within his heart...'

The mystics continuously tell us about the Word, the Shabd, the Logos, the Kalma or Holy Spirit. They want us to experience this truth within, and the way to achieve this is to focus the attention and live in conscious remembrance as we seek the Lord – practicing the Presence with every breath, as Brother Lawrence has reminded us. A very high ideal, but the mystics tell us that the Lord wouldn't have granted us this opportunity if we couldn't reach our objective.

Hafiz tells us how to do it:

Picture the face of your Beloved becoming your face, and His body fitting on you like a coat you won't take off again.

Don't move so fast now, when such a rare kiss is being offered, for what lips can really connect with a body wired to a mind that is darting about in a manic hurry?

From this new perspective, look inside the Heart you have sought so long to be near. Try and go deep into it. Is it not your own, and mine too?

Truth is simple, the mystics tell us. We need to keep our objective in view and work toward that objective – to make a plan, walk the path that calls to us and keep trying, even when we feel our efforts are of no avail. It is His promise that matters, and the Lord will fulfill his responsibility and take us home if we simply continue to try.

Rumi puts it beautifully:

> We become reflected light... Listen to your
> essential self, the Friend. The morning wind
> spreads its fresh smell. We must get up
> to take that in, that wind that lets us live.
> Breathe, before it's gone.

Remember that wonderful poem, Footprints in the Sand? This is the way the Lord treats each one of us, for our souls are precious to Him.

> One night I had a dream. I dreamed I was
> walking along the beach with the Lord and
> across the sky flashed scenes from my life.

> For each scene I noticed two sets of
> footprints in the sand, one belonged to me
> and the other to the Lord.

> When the last scene of my life flashed before
> us, I looked back at the footprints in the sand.

*I noticed that many times along the path of
my life, there was only one set of footprints.*

*I also noticed that it happened at the very
lowest and saddest times in my life.*

*This really bothered me and I questioned the
Lord about it.*

*'Lord, you said that once I decided to follow
you, you would walk with me all the way,
but I have noticed that during the most
troublesome times in my life, there is only one
set of footprints.*

*I don't understand why in times I needed you
most, you should leave me.'*

*The Lord replied, 'My precious, precious
child. I love you and would never, never leave
you during your times of trial and suffering.*

*When you saw only one set of footprints, it
was then that I carried you.'*

Even though the Mystics tell us that the Truth is
simple, our life seems complicated with all of its
twists and turns. We may get discouraged when
things don't go 'our way'. But the mystics and

saints share that everything that happens is due to our past actions, and we are reaping what we have sown. Rumi puts it this way:

Life smoothes us, rounds, perfects, as does the river the stone, and there is no place our Beloved is not flowing – though the current's force you may not always like.

As human beings we tend to question and analyze everything that crosses our path. We expect results from our efforts, and when they don't seem to be forthcoming, we perhaps get frustrated, angry or discouraged.

On the spiritual path, the mystics say results are not in our hands. What is in our hands is the effort we make. The results are in the Lord's hands – He knows best.

So what can we do?

We say, 'Knock knock'.
The teacher says, 'Who's there?'
We say, 'I don't know – help!'

Brother Lawrence gives us this advice:

Concentrate on keeping your mind in the presence of the Lord. If it sometimes wanders

and withdraws itself from Him, do not let it
upset you. Confusion serves rather to distract
the mind than to recollect it; the will must
bring it back calmly.

What good advice – simply trying to keep the mind
aware of the Lord's presence in each moment. We
all know how the mind wanders continuously, but
we can try to bring the attention back to that center
still point, where we feel His presence. Every step
we take in His direction opens the heart. There
is a wonderful saying that goes something like 'I
lift my heart to God and grace is poured.'

In Rumi's *Book of Love* we find this encouraging
statement:

Keep walking, though there's no place to get to.
Don't try to see through the distances.
That's not for human beings.
Move within...

Once we understand the basic truth, find a teacher
and start walking our chosen path, our lives
expand from a confining outer existence to one of
inner exploration and discovery! The mystics say
that we will start to go beyond simply 'knowing'
to being an active participant in the higher Truth.

Coleman Barks shares a little about Rumi when he says:

Jelaladdin Rumi was one of those conductors of knowing and being. He was an enlightened human being, realized – whatever you want to call those who get to be deeply themselves. Rumi was completely focused on feeding the soul – on the inner path – yet using our human condition as a teaching tool. There is little one can SAY about love. It has to be lived, he says, and it is always in motion.

We keep walking, day by day, moment by moment, yet with a new direction in our hearts. We are seeking the Beloved. We are seeking the eternal Truth. We are seeking oneness with the Lord.

Rumi reminds us:

This is NOW, NOW is. Don't postpone till then. Sit at the head of the table. Dip your spoon in the bowl. Seat yourself next to your joy!

The Lord, in a profound act of incredible kindness bestowed upon all of us a human birth. And the mystics say that He is now gathering us into His loving arms to help us experience and appreciate our spiritual heritage. You can almost hear the

Beloved saying 'You are mine, and I love you completely.'

As Rumi says:

Let yourself be silently drawn by the stronger pull of what you really love.

Coleman Barks goes on to tell us that *'as one becomes a lover, duties change to inspirations. Practices become dance, poetry, creek music moving along. Finding a purpose for acting is no longer the problem. The soul is here for its own joy. It's by some grand shift of energy that we know Love. We have this great love-ache for the ocean... that is the subject here. For the longing builds and the real work (meditation, prayer, remembrance) grows more frequent.'*

Rumi tells us:

The Center leads to love. Soul opens the creation core. Hold on to your particular pain. That too can take you to God. Love moves away, the light changes. I need more grace than I thought.

15

The inner work

The saints say love is an open secret, but to experience this spiritual love the heart needs to expand. God is such a vast, unlimited Presence, how can we possibly understand with all of our limitations?

Bawa, the teacher of Coleman Barks, says:

Everything you see tells the story of God. Look at it. God is spread out filling the entire universe. So look. You exist in a form. God is without form. You are the visible example, the sun. God is the light within the sun.

The mystics say we are like a ray of the sun – never separate from the source. But we may question how can we possibly be a part of the Lord's greatness? Rumi shares our feelings:

I am so small I can barely be seen. How can this great love be inside me? The Beloved answers,

> 'Look at your eyes. They are small, but they
> see enormous things.... Stay bewildered in
> God, and only that.... God loves you is the only
> possible sentence.'

God has confidence in our souls! We have heard the mystics say that the Lord only gives and loves. What a boon to our searching and struggling souls. Now we need to do what the saints call 'the inner work.'

Rumi encourages us when he says:

> In the early morning hour, just before dawn,
> lover and beloved wake to take a drink
> of water. Be courageous and discipline
> yourself – work, keep digging your well.
> Don't think about getting off from work.
> Water is there somewhere. Submit to a daily
> practice. Your loyalty to that is a knock on the
> door. Keep knocking, and the joy inside will
> eventually open a window and look out to see
> who's there.

As seekers, we want to experience the fragrance of His love. And the mystics tell us the Lord wants nothing more than for the soul to experience its spiritual heritage. With grace and effort, the soul will start to become attuned to its inner voice and realize what the mystics have shared – the

Lord and his devotees are one. The flower is not separate from its fragrance.

Jonathan Star states:

> *There is a voice in us all that is ever-present, a voice that always sings its melody to the world. This is the voice of truth and certainty, the voice that lays bare the hidden mysteries of the soul.... The saints' every word is charged with purity and divine refulgence, and their poetry is a reflection of their own perfect state.*

The mystics tell us we must listen to this voice, stride forth and walk the path with sincere effort, knowing that God is there for us and with us each step of the way.

Saint John of the Cross has this wonderful story to share with us:

> *Saint John was a spiritual teacher to a particular group of Carmelite nuns in the hills north of Granada, and he would go there regularly to visit them.*
>
> *One day, the cook, a simple soul called Sister Catalina, asked him this question: 'Padre, why*

is it that the bullfrogs, which are in the garden near the water, throw themselves into the stream whenever I come near?'

'Because,' he said, 'it is in the water's depths that they feel safe. There they feel secure and protected; and, it is in this manner that we too should behave. We must turn away from created things and plunge into the depths, into the centre of all things, which is God – hiding ourselves in Him.'

The depth of love will be revealed only when we dive deep into our spiritual selves, shutting the outer doors of illusion and opening the inner doors of experience. We may think that as we make effort after effort to realize God, nothing has happened – why?

Saint John replies to this very question:

'Padre, since the Lord, whom my soul loves, is within me, why don't I find him or experience him?'

Saint John replies, 'The reason is that He remains concealed and you do not also conceal yourself in order to find Him and experience Him. If you want to find a hidden

*treasure you must enter the hiding place
secretly and, once you have discovered it,
you will also be hidden just as the treasure
is hidden. Your Beloved Bridegroom is the
treasure and the hiding place is your soul.
Therefore, if you are to find Him, you should
forget every worldly thing and hide in the
secret inner chamber of your spirit. Closing
the door behind you, pray to your Father in
secret. Remaining hidden with Him, you will
experience Him in hiding, love and enjoy
Him in hiding, that is, in a way that goes far
beyond all language and feeling.'*

In essence, we are placing our destiny in the
hands of our teacher, so that we can experience
God fully. This takes courage and trust in the one
who can show us the way.

Maharaj Sawan Singh tells us:

*If you have placed your destiny in the hands
of the Guru [teacher, Friend], he will and
must take care of you until the day of your
complete and perfect deliverance.*

What a promise! If we walk the inner way and
place our hand in His, he will and must take care
of the soul, until we rest in the lap of the Lord.

109

The mystics state that when the soul cries out for God, sincerely and incessantly, God has no choice but to run to pick the soul up!

Many times we may have thought, 'How can I possibly be worthy to go back to the Lord – I have no love in my heart.'

At our level of consciousness, it is hard to see and understand effort and the love present within the soul. A letter from a fellow traveler on the path has a helpful insight for all of us:

> I can just hear you saying, 'How do we know we're on the right track without measurable progress? At least with golf I can hit a good shot every once in a while.' How do you know you're not making progress? If you are intent on measuring progress, then do it this way. Are you following the vows (the steps your teacher has advised you to take) carefully? If you are, then this is progress. Are you regular and punctual in your meditation (prayer, remembrance)? That would be spectacular progress. Do you find yourself less whipsawed by the events of the world and in your daily life? Brother, that's the soul slowly being disentangled from the thorny bush of the world.

I'll tell you what the best progress is – this is one of my personal secrets: If you keep at your devotions, you will actually begin to enjoy it! You will look forward to entering the quiet refuge within yourself every morning. When I was a kid I used to hide in the coat closet when I wanted to escape from family upheavals. I loved the muffled quiet, the darkness, and the smell of mothballs. Meditation is my adult coat closet, and should be yours, too. As your mind settles down (it will, just give it time), you will enjoy moments of utter serenity. You will hear the pure sweet sound of the Word, the Shabd. And, most importantly, you will palpably feel the Master's presence within.

You will also find it remarkable how much a sense of love and devotion will grow in you. It's not a feeling you even want to talk about because it seems so personal. But it's there and continues to grow, and you feel the utmost gratitude.

You have mentioned to me that you feel like you're risking everything to follow the path and the Master. In a sense, you are. We're gambling that this path will lead us to the Lord in exchange for our love of the world.

This risk seems much greater than it really is. The path leads to a circle of love. Love goes from the Master to the disciple and then back to the Master. The reward of this love is too great to pass up.

You have said that you like to talk to me because you think I have it 'figured out'. This path is too subtle, too deep, and too long for anyone to think that they've figured it out. Besides that, each of us is walking through a karmic maze of our own creation. We never know from one moment to the next whether we will laugh or cry, or act the sinner or saint. The only one we should look up to is our spiritual teacher.

Here is the last secret. This path requires constant application. What do I mean by that? It means you have to weigh everything you think, say or do. In the beginning, this takes a lot of effort, as you might expect. Eventually, the Master will inculcate in you such a refined sense of conscience that anything you do outside the boundaries of the path will bother you. So, you have no choice but to constantly apply the principles of the path to your life. Ah, but what a sense of freedom this will give you!

The inner way takes work, application of the principles enjoined by our spiritual teacher, and adapting to a new way of living. Our thoughts change, our actions change, and our entire way of looking at the outer world shifts as the soul starts to turn toward its origin.

Maharaj Charan Singh tells us so beautifully:

The soul cannot help but love its own origin. So we have to lift the weight of the senses, of the mind, of karmas or sins, before we experience that love. And we feel real love when we go beyond the realm of mind and maya (illusion), when there are no coverings on the soul, when the soul shines, when it knows itself. Then it experiences the real love for its own Father, for its own origin.

Meditation creates love, it strengthens love, and by love it grows. The more you give, the more it grows. It grows to such an extent that we become one with the Father. That is love.

The saints tell us that the more effort we put into walking the inner way, the sweet cream of love will rise to the top and the Beloved will give us everything.

We may ask, why would God care so much about one feeble soul? Hafiz shares something profound:

My Beloved said, 'My name is not complete without yours.' And I thought, how could a human's worth ever be such? And God, knowing all our thoughts, and all our thoughts are just innocent steps on the path, then addressed my heart. God revealed a sublime truth to the world when He sang: 'I am made whole by your life. Each soul, each soul completes me.'

The saints tell us our soul has great value in God's eyes, and that we can experience Him consciously in our everyday lives.

Rabbi Harold Kushner shares:

When your life is filled with the desire to see the holiness in everyday life, something magical happens: ordinary life becomes extraordinary, and the very process of life begins to nourish your soul!

And John H. Vincent says:

Reach up as far as you can, and God will reach down all the way.

16

The garden of love

Whether we consciously realize it or not, the soul walks in the garden of the Lord and we can smell His fragrance moment by moment once we tune in. The saints say the soul is of the essence of the divine and as love grows within, we will slowly realize we are truly spiritual beings.

This poem by Kabir describes the garden, and how the Lord looks after the garden of our life with every step we take.

The lake of love within me,
O Kabir, overflows its banks
And I can no longer live
Without my beloved Lord.
Strengthen the water channel,
Irrigate the seedbeds
So the plant of divine love
Can thrive and grow.

The lake of love within overflows;
Without the Lord, Kabir can live no more.
Vigilant, he never sleeps.
He controls the channels
That lead the water astray.
The lake of love within overflows;
Without the Lord, Kabir can live no more.

The well within is brimming
With water cool and pure;
There the world's
evil winds never blow.
Thus the lake of love overflows;
Without the Lord, Kabir can live no more.

I am, indeed, fortunate,
For the Lord, in his grace,
Himself looks after my garden;
and the garden does not have to face
The dreary decline of autumn.
Kabir, the lake of love overflows;
Without the Lord I can live no more.

My Master planted
The seed of divine love,
He husbanded the farm well,

He helped me remove the weeds
Of my wayward mind.
Now the lake of love overflows,
And without the Lord I can live no more.

Only the true devotee
Reaps a perfect harvest;
The rest try to pick up spilled grains
But fail to earn true benefit.
Those who reach Home
Enjoy the harvest of bliss,
Their efforts crowned with glory.
Their lake of love, O Kabir, overflows,
And without the Lord they can live no more.

Says Kabir: Listen, friends,
The praise of such divine lovers
I can never adequately sing.

The mystics tell us we are already in the Lord's garden, we simply need to reach that level of understanding and experience to recognize our true home. Muhammad Iqbal says:

We are like a rose with many petals and one
perfume. He is the soul of this society, and He

is one. We were the secret concealed in His Heart.

We are seeking the perfume of the Beloved – the fragrance that will fill us completely. In *Perfume of the Desert*, one of the stories tells us this:

The one eternal perfume is the one that smells of the Nothing of God. It is this perfume – this bliss and ecstasy – that all mystics seek to 'smell' because they know it makes them drunk on the Beloved and lures them on to realize their identity with Him. And once you have smelled that perfume, your life is ruined because nothing else will ever be as fragrant and your whole being becomes longing.

The mystics say that as we walk this path, the longing will build step by step, even though we must still function in the world.

Working and living in the world can be difficult at times, and life may seem full of thorns, but with faith and perseverance our spiritual lives will begin to blossom.

In the *The Flower Called Rose*, we find this encouragement:

*Even when the entire universe is full of
thorns, the heart of a lover will ever blossom
into beautiful flowers of remembrance of his
Beloved.*

Suddenly we will find ourselves living and flowing within the river of His love. This fragrance that the mystics describe is not only about scents or smells. The essence of His love injects every pore of our being, and the sweetness of His love becomes a feast for the soul.

There is a beautiful song that speaks of building that relationship as we walk through the garden with the Lord:

*I come to the garden alone
While the dew is still on the roses
And the voice I hear, falling on my ear
The Son of God discloses.
And He walks with me and he talks with me
And He tells me I am His own,
And the joy we share as we tarry there
None other has ever known.*

*He speaks, and the sound of His voice
Is so sweet the birds hush their singing;*

And the melody that he gave to me
Within my heart is ringing.
I'd stay in the garden with Him,
Tho' the night around me be falling;
But He bids me go; thro' the voice of woe,
His voice to me is calling.

And He walks with me and He talks with me,
And He tells me I am His own,
And the joy we share as we tarry there
None other has ever known.

Being a gardener, I love all of the references in spiritual literature to the garden. It symbolizes a peacefulness and tranquility – a lessoning of outer worries and a slower pace that helps us see a bit more clearly.

When you take the time to really look at a flower, you start to see the miracle of life unfolding. The Lord's creation has so much beauty to share with us. The saints say that now is the time to dive deep into the fragrance of His love. As Rumi tells us:

Love is a rose garden – take nourishment
from it!

17

A balancing act

Sometimes when we go through deep spiritual transitions, life becomes a balancing act. We struggle with finding a new rhythm between work, family, responsibilities and our growing spiritual awareness.

The mystics tell us that twenty-four hours in the day is sufficient time to organize our lives to accommodate everything – but it takes practice. And patience!

In southern Africa the Matabele people speak of *Gashle*, to go slowly. The saints and mystics tell us to slow down our pace, as spirituality is a gentle unfolding, a step-by-step process as our lives shift toward the inner truth.

In this century we are so used to instant results that our very expectations can block our way and hamper our efforts.

Stepping back, taking time to smell the roses, will allow the spiritual beauty to unfold naturally. And these experiences will remain with us and help us to stay balanced.

We may sometimes feel we have a foot in one world and a foot in another – it can make us feel disjointed and unbalanced. Rumi has these poignant remarks to share with us about the experience of being on the threshold of the inner worlds:

O lovers, O lovers,
Heaven's drum calls my spirit and says,
'It's time to leave this world.'
Look!
The camel driver has risen.
The caravan is about to leave.
He says, 'Forgive me for waking you...
But why, O pilgrim, are you asleep?
Before you and behind you
The camel-bells are ringing.
It's time to go.'

With each passing moment
A soul sets off to find itself.
From the stars,
Suspended like candles
From the blue vault of heaven,

Wondrous souls have appeared
And the Unseen has revealed itself.
The revolving spheres have lulled you
Into a deep sleep.

Beware of this floating life.
Beware of this weighty slumber.
O heart, seek the King of Hearts.
O friend, seek the Eternal Friend.
O watchman, be wakeful –
The whole city could be lost
If you fall asleep.

Tonight, amidst the shouts and din of the city,
Amidst the light of candles and torches –
Tonight this fecund world
Will give birth to eternity.
You were dust and now you are spirit.
You were ignorant and now you are wise.
The one who brought you here
Will bring you still further.

Don't be afraid – His flames are like
cooling water.
To give your soul life is His sacred duty,
To break your binding chains is His only mission.

18

Opening the heart

There is a beautiful couplet by Hatif-i-Isfahani:

Open the eye of the heart to see the soul,
so that you may see what cannot be seen.
If you turn towards the domain of love,
you will see all horizons as rose gardens.

The saints and mystics talk about opening the heart, so that the Beloved may be seated there. This means cleansing the vessel, being willing to explore new thoughts and avenues, choosing the Lord over the world, becoming a good human being in word and deed.

The mystics tell us that the time is now – we can't put off until tomorrow the work that needs to be done today. This is how we become a lover of God. Isn't this what the soul is seeking – to become immersed in the Beloved right now, while in this human body? The saints always encourage us and help us understand what awaits the soul who opens her heart to God.

Rumi shares in his poem, "A Mine of Rubies":

Last night I learned how to be a lover of God,
To live in this world and call nothing my own.
I looked inward
And the beauty of my own emptiness
Filled me till dawn –
It enveloped me like a mine of rubies.
Its hue clothed me in red silk.
Within the cavern of my soul
I heard the voice of a lover crying,
'Drink now! Drink now!'
I took a sip and saw the vast ocean –
wave upon wave caressed my soul.
The lovers of God dance around
And the circle of their steps
Becomes a ring of fire round my neck.
Heaven calls me with its rain and thunder –
A hundred thousand cries
Yet I cannot hear...
All I hear is the call of my Beloved.

Rumi brings up several important points in this poem. When we start to empty the self of I, me and mine, the soul has room to expand and open the heart to an ever-increasing emptiness of 'self' so God can pour in His love. The mystics say that this is when we begin to feel and experience the depth of God's love, in that emptiness.

Then Rumi says to drink now! The mystics tell us that only this moment belongs to us – the past is the past, we can learn from it but it is like a dream; the future is in God's hands; the present – think positive thoughts and do positive actions. It is not easy to step out of our old skin of ideas and habits. But if we realize that the soul is simply a traveler passing through this life, it will help us to keep going with the flow.

A Hadith of the Prophet encourages us to be a passerby:

Be in this world as if you are a traveler, a passerby, with your clothes and shoes full of dust. Sometimes you will sit under the shade of a tree, sometimes you will walk in the desert. Be a passerby always, for this world is not your home.

This is not always easy to do – to feel we are simply a traveler. Everything about our life seems so permanent. But when we look at the big picture, we see that we live in a rented house for a set number of years, have a fixed number of breaths allotted to our lifespan, and will someday leave all that we know in this outer world of existence.

Sadi has this wisdom to share:

One night in the desert of Faid, I fell asleep. A camel driver shook me awake and said, 'Get up now! The bell is ringing! Do you want to be left behind? I too would like to sleep like you but the desert stretches ahead. How will you reach the end of the journey if you sleep when the drum of departure beats?'

Happy are those who have packed their bags before the beat of the drum! Those asleep by the road do not lift their heads and the caravan passes out of sight.

Now is the time to sow the seeds of the harvest you want to reap. Strive now, when the water does not reach beyond your waist; do not wait until the flood has raced over your head.

Listen to the advice of the wise today... Value your soul as priceless. Do not waste your time in regret; opportunity is precious and time is a sword.

19

Knowledge and experience

The mystics say it is important to remember that the Lord and his devotees are one. The flower is not separate from its fragrance; the rays are not separate from the sun; the drop is not separate from the ocean.

We want to know everything, and we go to great lengths to analyze, question and seek answers. The mystics tell us it is more important to repeat the name of God, for that will give us experience which is beyond what knowledge can offer.

There is a wonderful story that illustrates this. It is the story of the Banshee and the Saintly Leprechaun:

Most people know what a leprechaun is, but some might not know about banshees. In Ireland, the banshees are women spirits who haunt the woods and forests at night, loudly lamenting and crying for their beloveds.

*Once when I was very little I heard one
from the woods outside the convent where I
boarded. It was a terrible sound, which both
broke the heart and sent shivers up the spine.
And I have often thought since of the love of
the banshee who would yearn for her Lord
the whole night, under the dark tresses of the
forest trees, when I was asleep. If only I had
that devotion to my Lord.*

*Well the story goes that a banshee was
walking one day along a country road when
she happened upon a saintly leprechaun
who never was. He was leaning on a gate
looking wistfully into the sky taking no notice
of anyone. Every now and then he would let
out a deep sigh and join his hands together in
prayer.*

*The banshee was touched by all this and,
walking over, she asked the little man what it
was he was after doing, leaning on the gate
and looking so wistful.*

*The saintly leprechaun replied, 'O banshee, I
am waiting for the grace of the Lord.'*

*Later that same day as the light was fading
and the night hardly a mile off, the banshee*

happened to pass that way again. This time she saw the leprechaun was digging a large hole in the ground.

'O what are you digging for, little man?' she asked.

The leprechaun turned around and said, 'For His grace, O banshee.' Then he began to dig in earnest again, quite forgetting her presence in a moment.

That night when the moon was high and the banshee was off on her way to cry for her beloved Lord, she came upon the saintly leprechaun again. This time he was frantically searching in the bushes, his poor hands were all scratched and bleeding from the thorns, but the more he didn't find what he was looking for, the more he looked for it.

'O little man,' said the banshee, 'what are you searching for?' The little leprechaun turned his eyes to her and they were all sad and worn with tears. 'O banshee,' he said, 'I'm searching for the Lord's grace.' And then before she could say a word he dived into the next bush and she couldn't see him at all.

Well, it was the next day after that that the banshee decided she would pay a visit to the poor leprechaun and see how he was. Because in truth she had spent night after night crying and weeping for her Lord and had not found him. You see, true devotees always see the Lord in each other and so are a great comfort to one another, and indeed one is attracted to another like a magnet to a needle.

The banshee had to jump in the air as a whole bookcase full of books on philosophy and science and all sorts of things crashed down on the ground in front of her when she arrived at the leprechaun's cottage.

'O Heavens tonight!', she exclaimed, 'the leprechaun's after going mad and is throwing the contents of the house out the window.' She saw the door was open and ran in as quickly as she could in hope of preventing the little man from doing anything he might later regret. She was just in time to see the radio flying out the window and the saintly leprechaun was just lifting up the television. 'O little man,' she called our horrified, 'stop immediately, for I'm sure it's not half what you're doing that you're rightly aware of.'

'O sister banshee,' said the leprechaun, 'please keep quiet, for I haven't the time to pass with you this minute, can you not see that I am busy?'

'O tell me only what you are doing and I shall be quiet,' pleaded the banshee (for whom curiosity had got the better of fear).

There was a terrible crash as the television greeted the yard. The saintly leprechaun who never was sat down and addressed the banshee with these words: 'Dearest sister, after making a diligent search, I have found His grace is everywhere, it pours on everyone's head like a great waterfall, but until we make room for it in our lives we cannot benefit from it.

While we are full of this world we can search forever and not find it, but when we weed out the unnecessary things in our life, we make room for it. A small one like me needs a small chair, a large one like you needs a large chair, similarly He needs a very big space to fill with His grace, for indeed there is a lot of it.

O banshee, if all the breaths you spent asking me questions were utilized in repeating his

name, your Beloved would soon come. Be not
curious about the doings of other devotees,
for indeed the actions of devotees mystify all
except the Lord. Do your own work and God
be with you.'

Knowledge is valuable, the saints teach, but only up to a certain point. It is experience that will propel us forward. Experience will build the faith and strength to help us let go of past ideas and beliefs and encourage us to remain open to what each moment might bring. In a poignant quote from Swami Chinmayananda, we read:

If a bud is not ready to end its present state,
How can it grow and unfold itself to become
a flower?

The mystics tell us that all four legs of a chair are needed for it to remain in balance. Each person has a different set of circumstances in life, so one must experience the best ways and means to stay balanced throughout life. The four legs of balance will be unique to each person – patience, a good moral life, practice, compassion, gratitude – choose what will allow your soul to shine!

The mystics tell us that logic and love do not mix. They say everything must have a logical conclusion, and knowledge will definitely help us to a degree, but only experience will build the firm foundation from which love will grow.

By turning inward and exploring what lies within, the mystery of knowing and being will become clear. The saints say we may read all of the scriptures or literature available, hear every discourse or sermon, but until we put the teachings into practice, knowledge will lead us nowhere.

For example, continuing to read all of the recipes in a cookbook over and over again will not take care of the hunger we feel. Ingredients have to be purchased and cooked to satisfy our appetite. We could read a train schedule over and over but will not reach our destination simply by reading. The destination can be reached when we actually purchase a ticket and board the train. Kabir says:

Reading volume after volume,
Men tire themselves to exhaustion,
But not one becomes
a real scholar;
Who learns the one word 'love'
Is the truly learned one.
Put aside your scriptures, O Kabir.

All the world reads,
But reads in vain
If love's divine pain
Has not sprung in your heart.
Futile are your efforts
To meet the Lord
Through reading and reciting.
He who reads the one word 'Beloved'
Is the truly enlightened one.

The saints and mystics tell us we can help to mold our consciousness, change our habits and create an atmosphere that will allow the spiritual path to unfold. Our teacher will set the guidelines, and then we must act.

In *Living Meditation* we read:

Whatever we are today, it is the result of what we thought and did in the past. By the same rule of cause and effect, what we are to become in the future will be determined by what we think and do right now, today. Through our consciousness, our discrimination, we can choose at every moment to make a difference now, in this life, not only for the rest of our lifetime but

*for eternity. This is our privilege. This is our
challenge.*

We need to use our intellect to gain clear thinking,
and the mystics tell us that if we use the intellect
constructively, it can be a good friend on the
spiritual path.

Living Meditation continues with this statement
about clear thinking:

*Clear thinking is attained by practice, and
it is well worth cultivating it to help us
avoid falling into our own mind-traps. We
can help ourselves by reasoning things out
and thinking things through in the light of
the saints' spiritual perspective; by using
common sense to see if what we think seems
reasonable, logical and truthful; by checking
whether our conclusions will bring us closer
to or further from our spiritual goal.*

The mystics state that most of our knowledge is
conceptual. True wisdom comes through personal
experience and will provide an anchor to support
us through the ups and downs of life. By practicing
devotion to the Lord, worldly knowledge will fade
into the background and spiritual understanding
will blossom into love.

Rabindranath Tagore shares:

*Love is when the soul starts to sing and the
flowers of your life bloom on their own.*

This is the state every soul wishes to reach – its
flowers in full bloom immersed in the Lord's love.
There are no words to describe this state, the
mystics say. It must be experienced.

Dariya Sahib states:

*The one who practices the spiritual technique
Sees the Lord face to face.
Wondrous is the Creator who has designed
this body.
The human form is the top of the whole
creation.
You are the beautiful mirror, O brother;
The Lord reveals His Form within you.
See the path with the eye of the heart,
The Lord is revealing Himself within you.*

20

Heartfelt joy

The mystics and saints always tell it like it is – they reveal to us a path of struggle, effort and determination. But more importantly, they share the underlying joy that discovering the Lord's love brings to the soul.

The saints tell us when we are firmly seated in love's flow, there will be incredible joy. We all know love from the physical and emotional aspects of life, from parents, children, spouse and so on. But this is not the goal the soul is striving for.

The saints and mystics talk about love in its purest sense – the divine essence of God. How can we recognize this true love? Where is it found? How can we experience it?

Kabir has this beautiful verse to share called "The Story of Love":

The story of Love can never be told.
It is the sherbet of the dumb man
Who eats it and smiles silently.
Without any earth and without any seed
The tree of Divine Love just grows and grows
Heavy with a million radiant fruits
My Lover picks for me to taste.
When I calmed my mind
And entered my heart,
The love of the Lord
Leapt like a flame within me.
All my old ideas and beliefs
Just blew away like chaff in the wind.
It wasn't because of anything I am;
It wasn't because of anything I did;
But only because of Him and His wild,
miraculous grace
That I learned at long last the lesson of Love.
My coming and going have ended;
My mind has melted in the Mind.
Don't ask me to speak any more –
The story of Love can never be told.

Kabir is telling us that this love is to be experienced by our soul. The inner mystery will be revealed by the Lord's grace and his desire to gather us up in his arms and take us home.

Are we ready? To realize God is no small thing! Rumi shares:

O seeker,
These thoughts have such power over you,
From nothing you become sad,
From nothing you become happy.
You are burning in the flames
But I will not let you rest
Until you are fully baked,
Fully wise,
And fully yourself.

Rumi is stating that the Lord will not reveal himself until the soul is fully baked, fully ready to understand the truth. We may think we are ready, but only the Lord knows when the vessel is fit to receive him.

There is a story about a man who felt he was ready to experience God, and approached His spiritual teacher and told him 'I am ready for enlightenment – please give it to me.' His teacher answered that he was far from ready, but the man insisted. The teacher had him sit and close his eyes, and after just a moment, the man was writhing on the ground in agony, saying, 'Take it back, please take it away!'

When he opened his eyes and his teacher inquired what had happened, the man replied 'It was like being burnt by a thousand lights or rays of the sun – it was so bright that I couldn't bear it.'

The moral of the story is that we must trust God to know when experiences should come to the soul. If we are convinced that the path we follow is the right one for us, then we must sincerely give it our best effort and know results will come at the proper time. The saints tell us if we have firm faith in the Lord, He will definitely open the way for the soul to return home.

Rumi has another beautiful poem to share with us:

Do not despair
If the Beloved pushes you away.
If He pushes you away today
It's only so He can draw you back tomorrow.
If he closes the door on your face,
Don't leave, wait –
You'll soon be by His side.

If He bars every passage,
Don't lose hope –
He's about to show you
A secret way that nobody knows...
He gives and gives
Yet does not startle a single heart.

I love this poem, for it speaks of one of the hardest lessons to learn in life – patience.

We are sometimes so quick to complain that our spiritual growth is not happening fast enough, or that we don't feel anything changing. The mystics say it is for us to make the effort and then to leave the results in the Lord's hands. He alone knows what it takes to rebuild our foundation into one of love.

There's a saying that goes: *We can complain because rose bushes have thorns, or rejoice because thorns have roses.*

The mystics tell us to put on strong shoes with sturdy soles to deal with the thorns of the world. Keeping the attention on the fragrance of His love, saints say we will rise above the ever-shifting sands of time and space and feel the joy of discovery transform the soul.

Kabir shares this poem, "Castles of Sand:"

My mind, kindle within thee
The flame of love for the Lord;
They become free who take refuge
With loving surrender at his feet.
Be not enamored
Of physical beauty –
It is just a drop of dew
On a blade of grass,
A castle of sand
On the changing shores of the sea.
This precious human birth
You will not get again;
Your numbered days
Are slipping by in vain.
Kabir, the slave, has ascended
To the pinnacle of the fort;
From there, he calls all men
to the beat of drum to victory.

The mystics ask us to take life seriously, for
the time our soul has in this plane of existence
is extremely limited. Kabir says that the ever-
changing essence of time is slipping by so quickly
that we must search for the Lord while we are

in this human body. The soul is reaching for the nectar of the Lord's Name – the spiritual treasure that lies within. The mystics tell us that searching within will bring forth the joy – now. Now is the time to find the Lord.

Hafiz tells us:

The rose has flushed red, the bud has burst,
and drunk with joy is the nightingale.

The saints and mystics want our joy to be permanent and everlasting, tapping into the deep well of the soul and filling it with divine nectar. Remember what John Keats shared?

A thing of beauty is a joy forever;
The loveliness increases;
It will never pass into nothingness.

The teachings of the mystics and saints bring joy to our hearts, for living this way of life and following the path to the best of our ability will bring us full circle into the essence of the Lord's divine love.

21

The Lord's essence

Words are so very limited and can never express adequately what the divine essence of the Lord actually is and how the soul can experience it fully. The saints come to teach us the method, to show us the way and to help us understand our spiritual nature. As we follow their instructions, take action and walk the path, everything will open up to the beauty that lies within.

Kabir tells us:

I absorbed my attention within
And realized my true self;
The color with which I'm dyed,
That I know is fast, is true.
My mind and soul are imbued
with that brilliant color,
I am dizzy with joy;
But people say Kabir has gone mad.

These fools know not the divine hue
That pervades all living beings.
In a color that is constant,
In a hue that will never fade,
In that glorious flush of divine love
Kabir stays forever immersed.

This poem really speaks to the heart. First of all, the mystics tell us that this is a personal path, an intimate unfolding between the soul and God. We might find it hard to discuss or relate the joy we are feeling to friends who may not understand. But the Lord's color of love is a constant for the soul, and will never change.

As understanding grows, we will realize more and more that His love is the music that we dance to from moment-to-moment, breath-to-breath. Sultan Bahu says:

The bud of my heart would unfurl
Into a flower,
Were I to receive his Word,
Were I called to his presence.

So much depends on our attitude towards this gift of life. Each moment can be a joy for our soul

148

if we remain open to the possibilities and follow the flow of our teacher's advice.

Rumi has this great poem:

On a day when the wind is perfect
The sail just needs to open
And the world is full of beauty.
Today is such a day:
There is a breeze that can enter the soul.

To seek the source, the root of our being, the divine essence of the Lord, is no small task. The mystics tell us it is the 'Supreme Achievement', and there is nothing of value in this transitory world in comparison.

The mystics and saints tell us time and again that the kingdom of God lies within. We must therefore go within and turn all our attention and thoughts towards that inner focus – the third eye or tisra til, the gateway, the door to our true home. The mystics explain this is how we realize our true selves and realize God.

Saints tell us that by turning our attention inward, we start to lose ourselves in the essence of the Lord. It is a gradual unfolding of infinite beauty for the soul. Rumi shares these thoughts:

Lose yourself,
Lose yourself in this love.
When you lose yourself in this love,
You will find everything.
Lose yourself, lose yourself.
Escape from the black cloud
That surrounds you.
Then you will see your own light
As radiant as the full moon.
Now enter that silence.
This is the surest way
To lose yourself...

We find our lives becoming one of discovery and experience, our understanding grows and we start to see more clearly what a gift this human form is.

Guru Amar Das Ji says that our body is the temple of God:

This body is truly the Hari mandir. Hari
meaning Lord, and mandir means the place
where the Lord resides. So the Lord Himself
is within each one of us.

The saints say this human body is a laboratory where we undertake research for reunion with the

Lord, for it is only through this precious human form that we can realize God. They tell us that the Lord is in the soul, and the soul is in the Lord.

What is the Lord's true essence?

The mystics explain that the Lord's divine essence is the Word, Shabd, Logos, Audible Life Stream that we have been discussing. By following our teacher's advice and making the effort, the soul will get tuned into that Word, the creative power that pervades the entire universe.

One mystic has shared that the uncovering of the soul is the discovering of God.

What a journey!

There is a wonderful story I would like to share about a Master and his disciple. I am paraphrasing from memory, so here goes:

The Master and his disciple were walking back to his house one day and they were discussing some of the great lady saints – such as Rabia Basri, Mira Bai and Sahjo Bai. Their devotional qualities and intense love for the Lord, their lives, focus and poetry were topics of discussion. The disciple mentioned

*how rare and precious was their devotion to
the Lord.*

*The teacher paused and stopped and turned
to her and said, 'Why not you?'*

*She stuttered, being stunned and taken back
by her teacher's words and replied that she
didn't have the devotion or the love or the
qualities of those great saints – how could she
possibly be compared to them? How could
she possibly achieve what they had achieved?*

*Again the Master stopped and looked her
squarely in the eyes and said, 'Why not you?'*

*All the way back to her house, she thought
about her teacher's words, and slowly and
surely started changing her life to emulate
those great saints they had been discussing.*

Think about it – why not us?

The saints and mystics tell us that we can do it!
Whatever path we choose to follow, wherever we
choose to worship the Lord – church, mosque,
synagogue, temple or even in our own home – if
we listen to what our teacher is telling us and
follow his/her example, we will find our way back

to God. We need that personal experience to give us the conviction that we are on the right track.

There is a wonderful example given by Faith Singh that helps us visualize:

Imagine for a moment that you are in a wilderness, without any shelter, and it is bitterly cold. As your body gets colder and colder, you put on more and more layers of protective clothing. The sun may be shining, but its warmth is not reaching you. You dare not take off even one layer, even though other people keep telling you that the sun is, in fact, warm. You can't feel it yourself. You don't trust them. You are chilled to the bone from the biting cold.

But then you happen upon a sheltered spot where, for a moment, the sun's warmth does penetrate. Enjoying the relief, you stay there for a while. Eventually you cautiously remove one layer of clothing. You allow yourself to feel the warmth of the sun. Your confidence builds and you take off still further layers as you delight in the power of the sun to revive your frozen limbs.

The discourse (teachings, sermon, advice) of a spiritual Master is that shelter where the warmth of God's truth first touches our hearts. Swathed as we are in the layers of the mind, only the truth, spoken by an adept who knows that truth, has the power and authority to penetrate the thick layers covering our souls.

When we attend such a discourse, our souls, lying petrified within us, come to life. They respond to the vibrant ring of the truth. They hear their own language. They hear themselves spoken of. They recognize their Friend. If the time is right, just one word, one phrase, can strike us with such force that from that day on our entire lives are transformed.

As long as we focus primarily on the material, the world of mind and matter, the soul's power remains subdued, latent and unknown. Like a child at a large gathering, the soul is inward and shy. But give it the company of its own kind and it revives – our hearts gladden. Then we say with conviction, 'Yes! That is who I am!' A spiritual being having a human experience! The core of us, our very heart, the wellspring of our being, has been ignored, unrecognized, neglected and in exile.

A Master's true spiritual message gives us the certainty that the spirit is the prime

reality – the soul of our life. It helps us
to know and experience this truth within
ourselves.

There are many examples of mystic teachers bringing the same message to the soul. Here is one from Isaac Ezekiel, in the book *Saint Paltu:*

His teachings were simple and convincing. He
asked people to know themselves, to realize
that the individual soul was a drop of the
ocean of the Divine Soul, and the purpose
of human life was to seek the reunion of the
two, the drop and the ocean.

How do we 'know ourselves', we might ask? Effort, effort, effort – following our teacher's advice and realizing that it is love alone that will bring us to the Lord's door.

Maharaj Charan Singh shares:

...If you want to reach the Lord's home, only
your love and devotion will be considered.
Only someone whose heart is filled with
yearning for union with the Lord, with love
and longing for Him and restlessness to find
Him, will be privileged to return and merge
with Him. Most fortunate are they whose

hearts are filled with love for the Lord. Theirs is a great destiny. Indeed, we should celebrate their birth as human beings, for one day they will find peace in the lap of the Lord.

So, dear friends, as we begin our spiritual journey, stage by stage, step by step, we will find the soul returning to its final destination – union with the Lord. The mystics say that we will then fulfill the purpose of being born a human being. Such people are blessed with a great destiny.

Hafiz shares this final couplet with us:

Let us be like
Two falling stars in the day sky.
Let no one know of our sublime beauty
As we hold hands with God
And burn
Into a sacred existence that defies –
That surpasses
Every description of ecstasy
And love.

Thank you!

Quest for truth

What is it within ourselves that draws us to seek, to explore all avenues that may lead our soul to the Truth?

What drives us day by day into uncharted territory – a place where mind and matter are insignificant?

What is this inner urging that compels us to find the answers to the reason for our existence and to question whether a superior power (God, the creative energy) is present in our lives on a day-to-day basis?

What part of us is real and lasting?

How important is it for us to understand the purpose of the soul's journey?

What will the end result be?

The saints and mystics encourage us to go on exploring our questions. Enjoy unlocking the inner doors and discovering the truths that speak to the heart and soul on this personal journey into the depths of love.

Notes on poems, quotes and stories

*Occasionally I have added a few words in parentheses in the body of a quote – to clarify or add to the meaning of a term in the quote. These parenthetical words are **mine**, not the author being quoted.*

TRANSITIONS

Hints of your beauty   Hafiz; Daniel Ladinsky, *A Year with Hafiz*.

1: AWAKENING

What is this precious love   Hafiz; Daniel Ladinsky, *The Gift*.

Our spiritual development   Maharaj Sawan Singh, *Spiritual Link Magazine*, August 2009.

I would like to remove   Hafiz; Daniel Ladinsky, *A Year with Hafiz*.

The reality of life   Baba Jaimal Singh, *Spiritual Letters*.

For the past twenty years   Author unknown, *Spiritual Link Magazine*, Spring 2020.

Rare is the human birth   Kabir in the Adi Granth.

My home is within you   Maharaj Sawan Singh, *Dawn of Light*.

2: DESTINY

Awareness is the state   Dictionary definition quoted in Wikipedia.

You love that you   Mikhail Naimy, *The Book of Mirdad*.

Mystics – gardens of wish-fulfilling trees   Judith Sankaranarayan, *Many Voices, One Song*.

Set no limits   Mikhail Naimy, *The Book of Mirdad*.

If you want your dream   Donovan, "Little Church" lyrics.

Love is the great work   Hafiz; Daniel Ladinsky, *The Gift*.

I have read in books   Maharaj Charan Singh, *Spiritual Discourses*, Vol. 2.

3: THE WORTH OF A SOUL

You are more precious   Rumi; James Fadiman, *Essential Sufism*.

Man is a God   Mikhail Naimy, *Book of Mirdad*.

O lovers, where are you going?   Rumi; Jonathan Star, *In the Arms of the Beloved*.

God is one   Maharaj Charan Singh, *Thus Saith the Master*.

We have been in love   Hafiz; Daniel Ladinsky, *I heard God Laughing*.

When the mind is consumed   Hafiz; Daniel Ladinsky, *The Gift*.

Remember that the key   Mikhail Naimy, *The Book of Mirdad*.

4: THE KEY

The clear night sky   Hafiz; Daniel Ladinsky, *A Year with Hafiz*.

A spirit that lives   Rumi; Coleman Barks, *Bridge to the Soul*.

5: SHIFTING INTO LOVE

Rise up nimbly   Rumi; Coleman Barks, *The Illuminated Rumi.*

We always see   Rumi; Coleman Barks, *The Illuminated Rumi.*

Consider the words   Mark Nepo, *The Exquisite Risk.*

The Lord has blessed us   Maharaj Charan Singh, *RS Greetings Magazine*, Spring 1992.

6: MEETING THE FRIEND

To be in the human body   Maharaj Charan Singh, *RS Greetings Magazine*, Spring 1992.

The call is present   Maharaj Charan Singh, *RS Greetings Magazine*, Spring 1992.

God wants to be known   John Ortberg, *God Is Closer than You Think.*

Perhaps only a small handful   Andrew Harvey and Eryk Hanut, *Perfume of the Desert.*

When the desire for the friend   Shaikh Abu-Saeed Abil-Kheir; Vraje Abramian, *Nobody Son of Nobody* – quoted in Hector Esponda Dubin, *Living Meditation.*

7: THE HEART OF LOVE

Mystics say that the nature   John Davidson, *Treasury of Mystic Terms*, Vol. 2.

Dear mind, such a traveler   Rumi; Coleman Barks, *The Big Red Book.*

Love is the richest   Maharaj Sawan Singh, *Philosophy of the Masters,* Vol. 2.

A place where there is love   Maharaj Sawan Singh, *Philosophy of the Masters*, Vol. 2.

I give this advice   Saint John, quoted in *Philosophy of the Masters*, Vol. 2.

The meaning of 'prem'   Maharaj Sawan Singh, *Philosophy of the Masters*, Vol. 2.

The rays have merged Guru Arjan Dev, quoted in *Philosophy of the Masters*, Vol. 4.

8: PATIENCE, PERSEVERANCE AND PRACTICE

A hermit was living alone   Dalai Lama; Leshe Thupten Jinpa, *Perfecting Patience*.

The two most powerful warriors   Leo Tolstoy, *War and Peace*.

If we want to live   M.J. Ryan, *The Power of Patience*.

When you encounter   Scott Curran.

Perseverance, sometimes   Oxford Dictionary Definition.

Brother, it takes both   Maharaj Charan Singh, *Spiritual Perspectives*, Vol. 2.

If you take one step   Bhai Gurdas, quoted in Hector Esponda Dubin, *Living Meditation*.

God's grace is always there   Maharaj Charan Singh, *Spiritual Perspectives*, Vol. 2.

I confided in the wind   Hafiz; Geoffrey Squires, *Hafez, Translations and Interpretations*.

9: TRUE DEVOTION

We should sit at the feet   Rumi, quoted in *Philosophy of the Masters,* abridged edition.

Devotion is a spontaneous   Maharaj Sawan Singh, *Philosophy of the Masters,* Vol. 2.

If you embrace his name   Eknath; Judith Sankarnarayan, *Many Voices, One Song.*

Ceaselessly repeat the name of God   Samarth Ramdas; Jonathan Star, *In the Arms of the Beloved.*

He himself makes it possible   Maharaj Sawan Singh, *Philosophy of the Masters,* Vol. 1.

While we are alive   Maharaj Charan Singh, *Spiritual Discourses,* Vol. 1.

10: SETTING THE GOAL

Many years ago, a young man   John Leeming, "The Song of Sant Mat."

11: WALKING THE TALK

What is the difference   Hafiz; Daniel Ladinsky, *I Heard God Laughing*.

Happiness and freedom   Epictetus and Sharon Lebell, *The Art of Living*.

Strive, struggle, grapple   Rumi, quoted in Hector Esponda Dubin, *Living Meditation*.

There is no mode   Brother Lawrence; Father Joseph de Beaufort, *The Practice of the Presence of God*.

In the beginning   Brother Lawrence; Father Joseph de Beaufort, *The Practice of the Presence of God*.

12: HONEST EFFORT

In the marketplace   Baba Kuhi of Shiraz; Andrew Harvey and Eryk Hanut, *Perfume of the Desert*.

Constantly mastering his mind   Bhagavad Gita; Andrew Harvey and Eryk Hanut, *Perfume of the Desert*.

To follow the path   Hector Esponda Dubin, *Living Meditation.*

Seek ye first The Bible, *Matthew*, 6:21.

Do you want knowledge   Nasruddin; Andrew Harvey and Eryk Hanut, *Perfume of the Desert.*

You know a dream   Garth Brooks, "The River" (1992).

13: LOVE GIVES THE SOUL WINGS

If you would stand well   Richard Rolle, quoted in *Science of the Soul Magazine*, December 1983.

In the beginning   The Bible, *John*, 1:1.

(The soul) becomes so free   Hafiz; Daniel Ladinsky, *I Heard God Laughing.*

No one can untie the knot   Richard Rolle, quoted in *Science of the Soul Magazine*, December, 1983.

Unfold your own myth Rumi; Coleman Barks, *Rumi's Book of Love.*

14: TRUTH IS SIMPLE

Known in different religions   Glossary, *Spiritual Discourses*, Vol. 2.

He who cherishes the Word   Guru Arjan Dev, quoted in *Spiritual Link Magazine*, July 2014.

Picture the face   Hafiz; Daniel Ladinsky, *A Year with Hafiz*.

We become reflected light   Rumi; Coleman Barks, *Rumi's Book of Love*.

One night I had a dream   Author unknown, "Footprints in the Sand."

Life smoothes us   Rumi; Daniel Ladinsky, *Love Poems from God*.

Concentrate on keeping your mind   Brother Lawrence, quoted in Hector Esponda Dubin, *Living Meditation*.

Keep walking   Rumi; Coleman Barks, *Rumi's Book of Love*.

Jelaladdin Rumi was   Coleman Barks, *Rumi's Book of Love*.

This is NOW   Rumi; Coleman Barks, *Rumi's Book of Love*.

Let yourself be   Rumi; Coleman Barks, *The Illuminated Rumi*.

The Center leads to love   Rumi; Coleman Barks, *Rumi's Book of Love*.

15: THE INNER WORK

Everything you see   Bawa, teacher of Coleman Barks, in the introduction to Rumi, *Bridge to the Soul*.

I am so small   Rumi; Coleman Barks, *The Essential Rumi*.

In the early morning hour   Rumi; Coleman Barks, *Rumi's Book of Love*.

There is a voice   Jonathan Star, *In the Arms of the Beloved*.

Saint John was a spiritual teacher   Saint John of the Cross, quoted in *Spiritual Link Magazine,* May 2010.

Padre, since the Lord Saint John, "The Spiritual Canticle", Stanza 1.9 quoted in *Spiritual Link Magazine,* May 2010.

If you have placed Maharaj Sawan Singh, *Spiritual Gems.*

I can just hear you saying Author unknown, *Spiritual Link Magazine*, May 2014.

The soul cannot help Maharaj Charan Singh, *Spiritual Perspectives*, Vol. 3.

My Beloved said Hafiz; Daniel Ladinsky, *A Year with Hafiz.*

When your life is filled Rabbi Harold Kushner, Meiji Stewart, *Relax, God is in Charge.*

Reach up as far as you can John H. Vincent, Meiji Stewart, *Relax, God is in charge.*

16: THE GARDEN OF LOVE

The lake of love is within me Kabir; V.K. Sethi, *Kabir, the Weaver of God's Name.*

We are like a rose Muhammad Iqbal, quoted in *The Flower Called Rose.*

The one eternal perfume   Andrew Harvey and Eryk Hanut, *Perfume of the Desert*.

Even when the entire universe   Anonymous author, quoted in *The Flower Called Rose*.

I come to the garden alone   C. Austin Miles, "In the Garden," song from 1912.

Love is a rose garden   Rumi, quoted in *The Flower Called Rose*.

17: A BALANCING ACT

O lovers! O lovers   Rumi; Jonathan Star, *In the Arms of the Beloved*.

18: OPENING THE HEART

Open the eye of the heart   Hatif-i-Isfahani, quoted in *The Flower Called Rose*.

Last night I learned   Rumi; Jonathan Star, *In the Arms of the Beloved*.

Be in this world   A Hadith of the Prophet, quoted in Andrew Harvey and Eryk Hanut, *Perfume of the Desert*.

One night in the desert   Sadi; Andrew Harvey and Eryk Hanut, *Perfume of the Desert*.

19: KNOWLEDGE AND EXPERIENCE

Most people know what   Quoted in *Spiritual Link Magazine*, January 1983.

If a bud is not ready   Swami Chinmayananda, quoted in *The Flower Called Rose*.

Reading Vol. after Vol.   Kabir; V.K. Sethi, *Kabir, the Weaver of God's Name*.

Whatever we are today   Hector Esponda Dubin, *Living Meditation*.

Clear thinking is attained   Hector Esponda Dubin, *Living Meditation*.

Love is when the soul   Rabindranath Tagore, quoted in *The Flower Called Rose*.

The one who practices   Dariya; K.N. Upadhyaya, *Dariya Sahib, Saint of Bihar*.

20: HEARTFELT JOY

The story of love   Kabir; Andrew Harvey and Eryk Hanut, *Perfume of the Desert.*

These thoughts have such power   Rumi; Jonathan Star, *In the Arms of the Beloved.*

Do not despair   Rumi; Jonathan Star, *In the Arms of the Beloved.*

We can complain   Alphonse Karr, *A Tour Round My Garden.*

My mind, kindle within thee   Kabir; V.K. Sethi, *Kabir, The Weaver of God's Name.*

The rose has flushed red   Hafiz; translated in 1897 by Gertrude Bell, quoted in *The Flower Called Rose.*

A thing of beauty   John Keats, "Endymion."

21: THE LORD'S ESSENCE

I absorbed my attention   Kabir; V.K. Sethi, *Kabir, The Weaver of God's Name.*

The bud of my heart   Bahu; J.R.Puri and K.S. Khak, *Sultan Bahu.*

On a day when the wind   Rumi; Daniel Ladinsky, *Love Poems from God.*

Lose yourself, lose yourself in this love   Rumi; Jonathan Star, *In the Arms of the Beloved.*

The body is truly   Guru Amar Das, quoted in Maharaj Charan Singh, *Die to Live.*

Imagine for a moment   Faith Singh, foreword to *Spiritual Discourses,* vol.2.

His teachings were simple   Paltu; Isaac Ezekiel, *Saint Paltu.*

If you want to reach   Maharaj Charan Singh in a discourse, referring to Soami Ji's shabd "Listen, dear soul."

Let us be like Hafiz   Hafiz; Daniel Ladinsky, *A Year with Hafiz.*

A thankful heart

This book has unfolded due to the grace and love of my Satguru, Hazur Maharaj Charan Singh and His successor, Baba Gurinder Singh. I can only lay the pages of the written word at their feet, thanking them for each thought and each breath of remembrance.

For all seekers of truth and spirituality, may something that is shared in these pages touch your heart with the desire to know and understand what stepping into the light of your being means to your soul.

Grateful acknowledgements

I am grateful to all of my spiritual family, who have helped bring this manuscript to you:

Cynthia Spring for her incredible artwork for the cover.

Anthea Guinness at Salt River Publishing for her patience, advice and help in so many ways to shape the final document and publish it.

Peter Korzaan, my husband, who was encouraging at every step.

And all of my friends who gave such a positive response to the idea of this book.

A heartfelt THANK YOU to everyone.

Warm wishes,

Gretchen xxoo

Appreciation

*T*hank you for buying
a copy of this Salt River book.

And thanks for telling your friends
to do so, too – the authors appreciate your help
getting the word out.

If you would like to help further,
we would love you to leave a comment
at Amazon, sharing your response
to any of the SRP books.

Available at Amazon.com
Discount at SaltRiverPublishing.com

Salt River Booklist

Global Library Books
- Janice Fletcher, EdD – *Teach with Spirit: A teacher's inward journey guide*
- Anthea Guinness – *The inner way: A mystic anthology of songpoems, stories, reflections*
- Anthea Guinness – *Wake up! if you can: Sayings of Kabir with reflections and mystic stories*
- Anthea Guinness – *A path of love: Talks with Soami Ji of Agra* – BOOK 1 *K
- Anthea Guinness – *Becoming a disciple: Talks with Soami Ji of Agra* – BOOK 2 *K
- Anthea Guinness – *Hidden treasure: Spiritual poems by Soami Ji of Agra* – BOOK 3 *K

Tuppany Books
- Shanan Harrell – *Stumbling towards enlightenment* *K
- Gretchen Korzaan – *The depth of love*
- Gretchen Korzaan – *Stepping into the light*
- Renata Mongillo – *Figure it out*
- Rosemary Rawson – *Coming of age* *K
- Elley-Ray Tsipolitis – *Butterfly kisses*
- Elley-Ray Tsipolitis – *Fly with eagles*

Pocketbooks
- Anthea Guinness – *Dawn has come: Songpoems of Paltu*

Beyond Borders Books
- Dyan Dubois – *Rajasthan suite memory* – a novel *K

New Moon Books for children
- Gretchen Korzaan – *Runt, the littlest donkey*
- Tia Pleiman, Village Voices series – *I am the rainbow, With my hands, Color in the book, In my dreams*

Eye of an Artist Books
- Greg Meyer – *Arizona places: Otherworldly and beautiful*
- Janis White – *A widow's journey: An odyssey of healing*

Independent Publications Salt River assistance with editing – and/or book design, composition, cover design
- Dyan Dubois – *Essence of fire*
- Rosemary Rawson – *Dark bread and dancing*
- Farida Sharan – *Dance with cancer*
- Chloe Faith Wordsworth – *Living in Tune* series, *Quantum change, Spiral up!* and all the Resonance Repatterning books

www.SaltRiverPublishing.com

Colophon

Typefaces: Bookmania (designed by Mark Simonson), Philosopher (designed by Jovanny Lemonad), Adobe Brioso Pro (designed by Robert Slimbach)
Software: Adobe InDesign
Book Design: Anthea Guinness of Salt River Publishing
Composition: Anthea Guinness
Cover Art, used with permission: Cynthia Spring
Cover Design: Cynthia Spring
Printer: KDP.com
Printing method: Print-on-Demand (POD) digital
Paper: Library quality

www.SaltRiverPublishing.com

Salt River

Salt River Publishing believes in encouraging artists and publishing professionals to come together and reach their empowered "Yes!"

Salt River was established as a no-profit publisher

- to help writers, translators, poets, graphic artists and photographers bring their work into publishable form and make 100% of the profit on their book sales
- and to promote, for free, the expertise of publishing professionals whose services an author might need when they have a book in the making

We publish books that inspire, encourage or entertain, including children's books – and books that deepen the understanding of mysticism.

Do you have one?

www.SaltRiverPublishing.com

Reader response
to Salt River books

"So many problems are spiritual in nature. And healing often involves finding meaning, purpose and spiritual uplift. The right words at the right time can turn a life around. Therapists and practitioners can point the way for clients who are seeking meaning; writers and artists have an opportunity to share in that work. Thank you, Salt River."

Made in the USA
Monee, IL
06 January 2021